WHAT MOVES US
THE LIVES & TIMES OF THE
RADICAL IMAGINATION

WHAT MOVES US
THE LIVES & TIMES OF THE
RADICAL IMAGINATION

EDITED BY
ALEX KHASNABISH & MAX HAIVEN

UPPING THE ANTI

FERNWOOD PUBLISHING
HALIFAX & WINNIPEG

Layout and design: Devin Clancy, Shelagh Pizey-Allen, & Max Haiven

Copyedting: *Upping the Anti* Editorial and Advisory Boards

Upping the Anti
Toronto, ON
www.uppingtheanti.org

Published by Fernwood Publishing
32 Oceanvista Lane, Black Point, Nova Scotia, BoJ 1Bo and 748 Broadway
Avenue, Winnipeg, Manitoba, R3G 0X3 www.fernwoodpublishing.ca

Fernwood Publishing Company Limited gratefully acknowledges
the financial support of the Government of Canada, the Manitoba
Department of Culture, Heritage and Tourism under the Manitoba
Publishers Marketing Assistance Program and the Province of Manitoba,
through the Book Publishing Tax Credit, for our publishing program. We
are pleased to work in partnership with the Province of Nova Scotia to
develop and promote our creative industries for the benefit of all Nova
Scotians. We acknowledge the support of the Canada Council for the
Arts, which last year invested $153 million to bring the arts to Canadians
throughout the country.
The editors would also like to acknowledge funding recieved from Mount
Saint Vincent University.

Library and Archives Canada Cataloguing in Publication

 What moves us : the lives and times of the radical imagination
/ edited by Alex Khasnabish and Max Haiven.

Includes bibliographical references.
Issued in print and electronic formats.
Co-published by: Upping the Anti, The Radical Imagination Project.
ISBN 978-1-55266-988-4 (softcover).--ISBN 978-1-55266-989-1 (EPUB).--
ISBN 978-1-55266-990-7 (Kindle)

 1. Radicalism. 2. Radicals. 3. Social change. 4. Social justice.
I. Khasnabish, Alex, 1976-, editor II. Haiven, Max, 1981-, editor

HN49.R33W53 2017   303.48'4   C2017-903168-6
                                            C2017-903169-4

Contents

PREFACE

Thinking in motion

Upping the Anti Editorial Collective

UPPING THE ANTI is a radical, volunteer-run journal of theory and action. Since 2005, the journal has provided a space to reflect on the state of political organizing in Canada, document grassroots social movements, and contribute to movement debates.

The root of the prevailing lack of imagination cannot be grasped unless one is able to imagine what is lacking, that is, what is missing, hidden, forbidden, & yet possible, in modern life.

— Situationist International

This a moment of immense movement. People are moving across the globe in boats, in trucks, and on their own feet. We know what moves this human migration—forced by terrors both human and natural, our world undulates with the stamping feet and racing hearts of fleeing people. Across the Mediterranean Sea, through the borders of South Sudan, over the Rio Grande, walking north, and fleeing the rising tide of white nationalism in the United States into the supposedly welcoming arms of our own colonial state. Why we move is not the question. We ask "what moves us?" to reflect on what it is that moves us to act, to reject the colonial narratives and meagre capitalist offerings that keep us in stasis.

Organizing is being in motion; it is constantly moving; it is breathless racing to carry out actions, coalesce communities, and fighting to win. We suffer our defeats and celebrate our victories but scarce are the opportunities to plumb the depths of our movements, to reflect on our political moment and to examine the strengths, weaknesses, limitations, and failures in our approaches. Once we begin to act, then, we need to ask, "where and how are we moving?" to deepen our understanding of where we are going and how we get there. Organizing is not only being in motion, but also assessing the particularities of our advance.

As an active publication by and for radicals for the last ten years, *Upping the Anti* has been a forum for movement organizers to have far-reaching conversations across sectarian boundaries in an attempt to answer these and similar questions and strengthen the links between socialist and anarchist organizing. That a small, volunteer-run, and reader-funded publication has lasted a decade is a testament to both the vision of the founding editors and the resilience of the shifting editorial collective and advisory board.

Upping the Anti's longevity also attests to the importance of space the journal offers for organizers to reflect upon their actions. The journal has become a de facto movement archive, a place where a decade's worth of actions can be critiqued and reassessed. Archiving political processes, discussing strategy and tactics, and assessing our own histories is something most radical movements simply do not have the capacity for. We try to capture the stories and struggles that won't make it into any history book. We want to catalogue the stories of what moves us now and what moved us then to use this information to push our movements forward, and to also keep a record of how hard we fought for social justice, liberation and emancipation. If we've demanded rigour from our writers, it is because we believe our movements deserve the most profound contemplations; if we've pushed our contributors to think deeper and question harder, it is because we believe the writing in our pages is important enough to strengthen and expand movements and inform future actions.

This special edited collection of essays is a co-publication between *Upping the Anti*, Fernwood Publishing, and the Radical Imagination Project—organizations that share a commitment to document and assess social movement strategy. At *Upping the Anti*, we pride ourselves on publishing grassroots theory—theory and praxis borne of movements and birthed in struggle—and have sought to seize ideas back from the academy and place them back in the hands of people. We are pleased to collaborate with the Radical Imagination Project, a political project positioned within the university that shares our commitment to reach beyond it.

While our task as activists and writers is to discuss the strengths and limitations of our strategies and tactics to dismantle systems of oppression and domination, it is also imperative to debate and offer meaningful political alternatives and radical imaginations. Let this text be one more small contribution to the struggle to not only ward off the matrix of domination, but to also open space for how we can form new social relationships and political communities; how we can transcend repressive boundaries, and build a world where direct democracy, mutual aid, cooperation, and social solidarity are the norm.

What moves us: The lives and times of the radical imagination

Max Haiven and Alex Khasnabish

MAX HAIVEN is Canada Research Chair in Culture, Media and Social Justice at Lakehead University in Northwest Ontario and director of the ReImagining Value Action Lab (RiVAL). He writes articles for both academic and general audiences and is the author of the books *Crises of Imagination, Crises of Power: Capitalism, Creativity and the Commons*, *The Radical Imagination: Social Movement Research in the Age of Austerity* (with Alex Khasnabish) and *Cultures of Financialization: Fictitious Capital in Popular Culture and Everyday Life*.

ALEX KHASNABISH teaches sociology and anthropology at Mount Saint Vincent University in Halifax, Nova Scotia on unceded and unsurrendered Mi'kmaw territory. A radical anti-capitalist and anti-authoritarian writer, researcher, and organizer, he is the author of *The Radical Imagination: Social Movement Research in the Age of Austerity* (with Max Haiven), *Zapatistas: Rebellion from the Grassroots to the Global*, and *Zapatismo Beyond Borders: New Imaginations of Political Possibility*. Find him at alexkhasnabish.com.

No one can doubt we live in radicalized times. When we started the Radical Imagination Project in 2010, we bemoaned the stagnancy of the political imagination trapped in the fetid, suffocating swamp of neoliberal austerity. Today, at the same time as inspiring movements for social and racial justice enliven our sense of possibility and grassroots power, radical right-wing, reactionary, and neofascist forces appear ascendant and the so-called "radical centre" of technocratic neoliberal austerity is far from vanquished. If anything, today the radical imagination is suffused with visions of deepening crises, even apocalypse. Has there been a more crucial moment to take stock of how we got here, to reflect on our successes and failures (and the spaces in between), and to redouble our efforts to dream together of other common futures? That is the objective of this collection.

Seven years ago when we began the Radical Imagination Project, a social movement research initiative based in Halifax, Nova Scotia, we were seeking to make use of the resources and (unjust) autonomy of our academic positions to "convoke" the radical imagination along with radical activists and organizers. We were, and are convinced that the radical imagination is something we do together rather than something we individually possess. It is the critical animating spark of robust and powerful movements for social change and it emerges from solidaristic encounters and collective experiences of challenging power. We were dissatisfied with most social movement research that only described the radical visions inspiring a given social movement at a specific moment in time and, in so doing, transmuted movement-based knowledge into grist for the academic mill. Instead, we set ourselves the task of experimenting with a method based on providing space, time, and opportunities for radical activists and organizers that they cannot or do not provide for themselves. We also wanted to study social movements as they sparked against one another, not just working with single organizations but a whole milieu of different initiatives and platforms, from student activism to prisoner solidarity, from queer and feminist organizing to membership-driven anti-capitalist organizations.[1]

Much activism and organizing is necessarily urgent—it responds to imminent threats and attacks. But what all too often gets left behind are the larger notions of how we might live together otherwise. How do we make time to cultivate together these collective visions of the possible? Without such visions, can movements truly be resilient, transformative, and powerful? What are the visions of possibility that animate and orient our struggles? How can we learn from each other to make our movements in practice worthy of the visions they seek to advance?

As our research unfolded through long interviews, community meetings, focus groups, and a lot of patient participant-observation, we came to understand the work we were doing with activists and organizers as intimately tied to the ways movements are produced and reproduced. In turn, we learned about the ways the reproduction of movements challenges or sustains (sometimes both) relations of oppression and exploitation that characterize society more broadly. Instead of telling a story about how and why movements succeed or fail (structured largely by dominant narratives and values concerning what "success" and "failure" mean), we came to see our work with movements as a process of learning to reproduce ourselves better collectively. We wanted to understand how movements, most of the time, dwell neither in the airy heights of victory nor in the mire of defeat but in the everyday hiatus between them.[2] We wrote about these and other themes midway through the project, in our 2014 book The Radical Imagination.

Since its inception, the Radical Imagination Project has evolved from an experimental research project into a platform for a much broader engagement with the radical imagination. We continue to do ethnographically-grounded social movement research, most recently focusing on how social justice organizers sustain their organizing work over the long haul and the lessons they have learned from this. But we have also developed ways for convoking and circulating the radical imagination beyond movement spaces. We organize regular free public talks with local and visiting activists and thinkers, an ongoing documentary film series at the public library, festivals, collaborative skill-sharing workshops, and free schools. We also collaborate with a variety of organizations locally and internationally to create spaces of encounter to work through the challenges and opportunities facing radical social justice movements today.[3]

As co-directors of the project, we grapple constantly with the question of what the role of the researcher in solidarity with today's social justice movements should be. Beyond adopting either a distanced, allegedly "neutral" posture of the outsider or integrating ourselves wholly into movements, how can research as a practice of rigorous, critical, grassroots inquiry explore, broadcast, and nurture the radical imagination?

The authors and interviewees in this collection are a few of the many comrades we have encountered over the course of this project. They are all, in one way or another, researcher-activists committed to radical conceptions and practices of social justice and social change. They have all had a significant impact on us and we've worked or been in dialogue with many of them, even before the project's outset. In this book we wanted to turn the research lens on researcher-activists themselves: what could we learn from their narratives of political awakening? What lessons did they draw from their years of experience as both organizers and as critical, reflexive, and systematic thinkers? What insights could they offer when asked not to disavow their own agency as radical and revolutionary thinkers and actors but to read themselves in as part of the world-changing struggles they have helped build up even as they think with them?

What has emerged in the following pages testifies to the effervescence of radical struggles as well as to the power of ideas, debate, and encounter when they are in the service of those struggles. This is a book for those who, like us, fluctuate between rage and despair when met with the conscription of theory and movement-based knowledge by the grey armies of academe. It is for those who, like us, struggle with whether research (even radical research) has a place in a "post-truth" world teetering on the verge of ecological collapse and resurgent fascism, particularly when so many other activities seem so much more worthy and urgent.

The perspectives collected here do not resolve these questions, they do not settle our doubts or reassure us that we are on the correct path and that righteousness, if not victory, is our due. They certainly offer no validation of research itself as a radical act or of disinterested academic productivity as inherently noble or worthwhile. We began this project with the understanding that, at least for those of us who live part of our lives within the university, we must disabuse ourselves of such dangerous and self-satisfying illusions as quickly and thoroughly as possible. We maintain this conviction today. But the insights collected here do seek to catalyze and inspire the radical imagination. Each in their own way offer tools for steeling our hearts, strengthening our resolve, and recommitting ourselves to radical struggle over the long haul.

For us, the editors, this book represents a partial view of our "undercommons," what Fred Moten and Stefano Harney[4] identify as those networks of solidarity, care, and critical community that run within, against, and beyond the university. While we and many of our contributors work in universities—some of us in very privileged positions—our first allegiances are to common struggles. We see one of our roles in those struggles in terms of what Moten and Harney call "study": the collective empowerment and joy that comes from the repossession of the university's literal and metaphorical resources in the name of our movements and communities. "Study" here means the cultivation of critical intellectual relationships and solidarities in spite of the institution and in the name of generating encounters, ideas, and practices that, in our terms, animate and accelerate the radical imagination. When we began this project in 2009 it was in the shadow of the globalized capitalist financial meltdown of the previous years and the "age of austerity" it ushered in. We wondered at the time about the state and fate of radical mass movements, so conspicuously absent in the global north, capable of contesting the increasingly brutal and exploitative status quo and we sought to leverage radical research as a way of convoking the radical imagination that is the vital spark of world-changing movements.

A decade later we have not emerged from that shadow. If anything, the darkness seems to have deepened and our moment seems marked by a more desperate and nihilistic spirit. We need not belabour the point that the radical imagination is needed now more than ever, as evidence that the globalized white supremacist, heteropatriarchal, imperialist capitalist order is in crisis abounds. Life in the ruins of the capitalocene[5] demands the willingness and ability to collectively envision and build alternatives to it, often, and increasingly, simply to survive.

In this context the imagination is everywhere being radicalized but not always in the ways we would hope. Collective liberation is only one possible orientation for the radical imagination. "Radical" doesn't actually mean perspectives we happen to like; it means perspectives that claim to get at the "root" of social problems and propose systemic solutions. The shrill, rapid, and recent rise of far right and openly fascist organizations in even mainstream electoral politics across the global north and west is one manifestation of the radical imagination gone wrong. In the face of a failing status quo, many who were led to believe that middle class belonging was owed to them have, through the cunning manipulation of their sense of "aggrieved entitlement,"[6] been turned toward racist, misogynist, authoritarian, nativist, and deeply reactionary political imaginaries. The global landscape is even darker than this, marked by an expansion of the ranks of those deemed disposable and the territories written off as sacrifice zones at the altar of capital. The crisis this time seems to have been seized, so far, by the "alt-right," far right, and neo-fascist forces.

What can those of us committed to and struggling toward collective liberation reflect carefully on and learn in this moment that could aid us in envisioning better ways forward? How can we cultivate and share our freedom dreams?[7] And, given that all our contributors are located within settler-colonies, how can we do so in right-relation to one another, to the land, and to the histories of violence and devastation that define the present moment?[8]

Searching for ways forward, the texts collected here offer us clues. They are the narratives of some of the most inspiring activists and thinkers we know, generated through protracted dialogue and engagement in a decidedly radical vein. In each piece, our collaborators were asked to consider and respond to two central questions, one about the birth and subsequent development of their radical consciousness, the other focused on their specific commitments in social change struggle. What you hold now is what they have offered back to us in hopes of moving us toward collective liberation. These diverse narratives of discovery, growth, and transformation are not the stuff of bourgeois melodrama or narcissistic self-valorization. They are the biographies of revolutionaries, critical political interventions bearing on some of the most pressing social justice issues of our time, and prisms through which to consider theories and strategies of social change that are all too often rendered abstractly.

It is our honour to present them to you.

Notes

1. See Max Haiven and Alex Khasnabish, *The Radical Imagination: Social Movement Research in the Age of Austerity* (London and New York: Zed Books, 2014).

2. See Max Haiven and Alex Khasnabish, "Between Success and Failure: Dwelling with Social Movements in the Hiatus," *Interface: A Journal for and about Social Movements* 5, no. 2 (2013): 472-498.

3. See http://radicalimagination.org for more information.

4. Stefano Harney and Fred Moten, *The Undercommons: Fugitive Planning & Black Study* (Wivenhoe, New York and Port Watson: Minor Compositions, 2013).

5. Jason Moore, *Capitalism in the Web of Life: Ecology and the Accumulation of Capital*, (New York: Verso, 2015).

6. Michael Kimmel, *Angry White Men: American Masculinity at the End of an Era*, (New York: Nation Books, 2015).

7. Robin D. G. Kelley, *Freedom Dreams: The Black Radical Imagination* (Boston: Beacon, 2002).

8. Leanne Simpson, *Dancing on Our Turtle's Back: Stories of Nishnaabeg Re-Creation, Resurgence and a New Emergence* (Winnipeg: Arbeiter Ring Publishing, 2011).

CHAPTER ONE

Explosive inheritance: Prison justice, spoken word, fearless love

El Jones

EL JONES is a spoken word artist, activist, journalist, and scholar. El is the former Poet Laureate of Halifax. Her collection of spoken word poetry *Live from the Afrikan Resistance!* appeared in 2014. She was the two-time captain of the back-to-back national championship Halifax slam team. She is a co-founder of Black Power Hour radio, the only prison radio show in Eastern Canada, and is a supporting member of By Another Name (BAN) founded in collaboration with Black prisoners to work for justice. In 2015, she was selected to be an International Resident at the prestigious University of Iowa International Writing Program. In 2016, she was selected as a recipient of the Nova Scotia Human Rights Award due to her community work. El was just selected to be the Nancy's Chair of Women's Studies at Mount Saint Vincent University. El gives honour to all the unnamed and unrecognized Black women who labour everyday in our communities and whose presence allows us to speak.

★

I grew up with a mother who compared the world to her father. When we went to fireworks displays, she would say, "nothing like Daddy's!" Over the years her descriptions of the fireworks her father made (illegally) in the back shed of their home in Trinidad became more fantastic. At Canada Day displays, my mother would praise the show, but then tell us how her dad could make faces appear in the firework pictures he constructed across the sky.

I have no problem believing his strange genius was actually capable of these unprecedented feats of radical imagination. Grandaddy's creations included the dragon mas at carnival, which came into his head as he saw a William Blake image of Dante's Inferno. Blending his Chinese heritage with the African struggle for emancipation, his mas embodied the struggle of Africans against colonial powers. Like the dragon mas, and unlike the exhibition of settler-colonial pomp in Canada, his fireworks displays were forged from and in resistance to colonial oppression. Educated as a chemist at German universities, he was denied a PhD because of his race. Returning to a pre-independence Trinidad where, in the words of V.S. Naipaul, there were "only 60 jobs," he could not find work as a chemist or a scientist. Thus began his career constructing fireworks in the backyard. This was decidedly not legal. This summer when I visited Trinidad, the family recounted an instance where there was an accidental explosion. My mother, the baby of the family, was singed in the blast. This, as I was told all my life by Mummy, accounts for her thin eyebrows. As this took place under British Imperial rule, with a government that feared terrorist attacks, the reports of Grandaddy's explosion caused much consternation. Mummy of course was coached to lie to the police as they searched the home for explosive materials, which Granddaddy had hidden in the oven. Grandmummy, a profoundly Methodist woman and as staunchly moral a Christian woman as ever walked the earth, calmly lied to the police while making her children's dinner.

My mother's accounts of Grandaddy's pyrotechnic prowess were not simply a child's worshipful exaggeration of memory. Rather, she insisted that his historic firework-making skill was an act of anti-colonial resistance. Denied the titles, jobs, and economic well-being he deserved, pyrotechnics represented the colonized person's refusal to knuckle under. Grandaddy's art was a constant act of rebellion and self-assertion. Like the calypso he sang on the eve of World War Two, which led to his being charged with sedition. The lyrics he sang from Patrick Jones' "Class Legislation" included:

> Class legislation is the order of the land
> We are ruled by an iron hand.
> Class legislation is the order of this land
> We are ruled by the iron hand.
> England and Germany teach democracy

Brotherly love and fraternity
And yet they leave us living here in this colony
Sans Humanité.

Along with being a pyrotechnic and calypsonian, Grandaddy was a trade unionist and political activist. He kept carnival alive through the war years, begging merchants for enough money for a small silver cup to be awarded to the champion singer. American military occupation in Trinidad during the war led to a craze for calypso, and seeing the tourist potential in carnival, the government sat at Grandaddy's feet to learn about the music and then stole it from under him, moved it to a more respectable area, and began excluding working class people and darker-skinned Africans.

Grandaddy's literally explosive legacy of anti-colonial resistance is surely the starting point for my own radical consciousness. Alongside his public and militant activity, however, was also the steady figure of Grandmummy, who was politicized in the way of African women through the centuries. While Grandaddy was rumoured to have the devil in him (again, literally) Grandmummy was a saint, who occupied her own pew at the front of the Methodist church, and sent my mother off to her education in England with a Bible and a hymn book. But it was Grandmummy who, when her son was born with what they called "waterhead," simply refused the doctors' advice to abandon him in a home. Bringing him home, she forced the schools—who on a small colonized island had no special education programs—to educate him and to teach him trades. He was her treasure, and his ability to know any hymn simply by its number in the hymn book was a valued contribution to the family. If Grandaddy provided the family history of radical action, it was Grandmummy's radical love that glued the family together. These poles of so-called militant activity combined with unwavering compassion to form my ideal of activism, and they guide me now.

I fortunately grew up in a house filled with books. As a child, the thick hardcovers represented the unopened world of adult mystery. My father's copy of the collective works of Oscar Wilde took up a prominent space on the bookshelf. At 13, visiting Trinidad to celebrate Grandmummy's 90th birthday, my auntie's copy of Frank Harris' biography of Oscar Wilde struck my eye.[1] Familiar with the name, I read it. I remember clearly Harris' quoting of Housman's "On Moonlit Heath and Lonesome Bank" and its lyrics about the hanging of a man:

There sleeps in Shrewsbury jail tonight
Or wakes, as may betide
A better lad, if things went right
Than most who sleep outside...

I quote those words from memory, as they made a huge impact on me at the time. Harris followed this up with Wilde's "Ballad of Reading Gaol":

I know not whether Laws be right
Or whether Laws be wrong
All that we know who lie in gaol
Is that the wall is strong
And that each day is like a year
A year whose days are long.

Again, I quote from memory words that hit me and that I memorized years ago. I was conscious at the time of reading my first real adult book, and that made the weight of these words of prison justice affect me profoundly.

So, that year when I had to write an essay in social studies class, where others chose topics like body image or photoshopping in magazines, I chose the conditions of women in prison. At the time, I didn't have a clear understanding of my racial identity despite growing up in a home steeped in anti-colonial narratives— that would come later in my life. This was the first political issue I understood as something unjust. I went down to the Elizabeth Fry Society to get information, to be met with confused questions about whether my mommy was in prison (now, understanding the racialization of prison, I can see this interaction through other lenses). I wrote an essay about the Kingston riots, and about how women should be able to raise their children in prison. I wrote about the cottage system and about Indigenous women. And while I was aware I was writing about something serious, at the same time, I don't recall this project as marking a profound revelation in my life in terms of desiring to become a lawyer or work with the legal system. It is in looking back now that I remember this assignment vividly and how it was poetry that led me to prison justice.

I became a spoken word artist by accident. I was attending graduate school in English at Dalhousie, a move which was accompanied by a radical shift in consciousness. I "became Black" in Nova Scotia, firstly because I encountered the first Black teacher I ever had. More than the teaching, it was his recognition of my Blackness that was transformative. My mother had a strong sense of family history and told us of all our relatives and the various ways they resisted racism, but she never put these stories in terms of race. One of these stories was about a great-uncle studying medicine in Scotland, and, since it is good luck to see a dark person first thing in the New Year, he enjoyed going from house to house getting food and drinks from the whole town. This kind of story was how my mother negotiated racism. She didn't talk about the isolation he must have felt, or what it must have been like as a Black man in a small village. To her, these stories were about how, given these circumstances, our relatives rose above, worked it, and succeeded. It was only once I grew up that I began asking the other questions—but why were there no Black girls in the school before my aunt?—that placed these stories in the context of historical oppression. Because of this, and because of growing up in a home with a white father, as a child I felt my claims to Blackness were uncertain. Coming to Nova Scotia, where I was not only recognized as Black, but where people expected me to do something about it (we have lots of kids who need tutors!) opened up my own history and identity to me. It was in the context of this recognition and claiming of my own Blackness, also accompanied by the growing consciousness of racism, that led me to become a spoken word artist. The words literally came to me in my sleep. The poem I wrote then, "White Neighbours," was all about the experience of growing up in white neighbourhoods and the double standards of racism:

> Kids in junior high school made fun of my mother
> Then they calling me in high school tryna get with my brother
> Make their parents freak, date him for a week
> Dump him, get another
> Then they talking bout how Black men be players
> Saying being faithful just ain't in our natures.

I talk about spoken word here because it was poetry that opened the doors to the prison for me. Poetry is a passport into communities, lives, places. When you do art with someone, when you share with them, in the words of George Steiner, "your heart has touched my heart with nothing in between." Radical political art is often labeled "angry" and "militant"—and I have no shame about the anger we should feel about our prison system—but its foundations are radical love. And it is this love, this sense of shared humanity—real recognize real—that for me breached the bars of prisons.

One thing people in prison tell me constantly is that if you have not been in prison, you cannot comprehend what it means to lose your freedom. We often describe things as being "like prison," but people inside make clear, if you haven't been there you will never understand. It's not just the material conditions, the deprivations, the hundreds of small humiliations, the difficulty in doing the most basic actions, the surveillance, the exploitation of labour—all things I have written on and that would take hundreds more pages—it is simply the condition of not being able to go where you want, call who you want, move how you want. One lifer told me "when I get out, maybe we'll go to the mall together or something, and you'll walk through the door, and you'll look back and I'll just be standing there, because I haven't used a door in decades." It's things like that, thousands of them. So when I say I am in solidarity with prisoners, I am not saying I know how it is. And if you think you know, people will check you right quick. Even with the people I am closest to, there are times when it just comes down to "I know you're trying to help right now, but you don't understand, and you can't understand, and I don't want you to understand because this world is too ugly." Even the words I'm using here. For a while I would use prisoner and inmate interchangeably, or say "people who are incarcerated." And then a guy inside told me not to call him an inmate, because inmates are people who accept their incarceration. Prisoners are here against their will, he said. Those kinds of small things illustrate how much we can never know.

So while I can say that I'm conscious of the connections between my anti-colonial histories and prison abolition, between enslavement and the number of Black men in prison, between silencing my grandfather for sedition and the iron hand of settler-colonial Canada, I can't say it's the same thing or an experience I can ever know. I think the most valuable thing I have experienced with prisoners is the move from radical consciousness to radical relationship. I was going to write that my only lesson of prison activism is "be real," and I think that's just what I meant. It's important to understand the prison industrial complex and to place it in context of histories of colonialism, genocide, racism, displacement, and state policing. I write a lot about just the basic facts of the prison system which a lot of people just don't know—things like if you move to a medium security facility, you have two weeks to find a job otherwise you're locked in your cell in work hours. So a lot of people end up working for CorCan out of desperation, which is a company that uses prison labour to make things like mattresses. They make you sign a contract to work there, so then you can't get out even if you find a better job. It's basically enslavement. I learn these things when they come up in conversation as part of a normal day for people inside. Then I write about it because we aren't even supposed to see or know that this is how our prisons operate. I think that's important, but really, it's the conversations and trust and friendship that allow me to do that work. And that's what I mean by radical relationships. At first when I was talking to people in prison I felt bad for talking about bad things in my week, because I would think, "at least I'm not in prison." But they wanted to hear, and be able to give advice, and be a friend, and talk like anyone else. That kind of stuff is important because we talk about prisons or prisoners like a system and not like it's made up of people. So I think being real and human with each other is actually really radical in this context. I often think about slave narratives, and why liberated slaves got up in front of usually white audiences and shared their most painful experiences. Why did they choose that rhetorical strategy to win freedom for the rest of their people? I think about what humanness meant to them and how those narratives were about being recognized as human. So I think a lot of what I've learned is just to be radically human with each other.

In a TED talk I gave a couple of years ago called "What I have learned from Prisoners," I said this:

> Another lesson I learned from a prisoner came when I was working with young men doing poetry. I knew the first name of one of the men, and it wasn't until he wrote me that I learned his full name, and then learned that he was a dangerous offender. I said to X that this offense was "over my line." I just couldn't bring myself to respond to him knowing what he had done. And later X told me this man was leaving for another institution and he said, "I went to say goodbye to him. I know you think he's disgusting, but he was a really good friend to me in here. He shared his food and he always encouraged me to write, and I know he did terrible things but he helped me out so I just told him to keep his chin up." And that moment humbled me completely. Because, again, here I was talking to people

about forgiveness. And what was being said to me wasn't about accepting or excusing horrible, damaging crimes, but simply saying that a person can have done those things and still have humanity. Seeing that humanity is not about supporting crimes or ignoring the effect on victims, but simply allowing ourselves to acknowledge that humanity is more complex than being good or bad or evil, and when we can challenge ourselves to see humanity even past our disgust, we are challenging ourselves to see beyond prison walls.

Sometimes I think the most important part of struggle is unconsciousness. G.K. Chesterton says that the heretic doesn't think they're a heretic, they think they're orthodox. They're right. I know when I started doing poetry, I had no idea you weren't supposed to say "white people" in a poem. It was just true. I was legitimately surprised at how offended and angry people got. Then I figured if it was making people so angry it was worth saying. It is the same thing with prison abolition work. I don't think getting on the radio and doing poetry with people in prison is particularly radical or frightening. I think part of getting engaged in struggle is just that sense we have of something being right, and because it makes sense to us, we just do it. It doesn't necessarily start as struggle. Also too, I think that as much as people see activists as critical, angry, confrontational, and so on, I think that you always have a belief—probably naïve—in the ability of people to transform society. So even though I critically understand colonialism and racism and state violence, some part of me is still surprised when there's backlash. What I'm trying to articulate here is that I don't know if it begins as struggle. I think it begins quite clearly—you have a sense of something wrong and you want to fix it. Then when people react, it becomes struggle against those forces. Then you start to struggle with yourself, because you realize what the consequences are. But if you can clarify your commitments, your sense of integrity, and the knowledge that you simply can't give up the work, then struggle coalesces into purpose.

Women have always done the emotional work in the struggle, particularly Black women. It's always the women in our communities holding it down. Eric Roach has a poem, "I Say it Was The Women," where he says, "It was the women who restored us."[2] He talks about how during and after slavery it was the women tending provision grounds, teaching, and loving. When I started doing poetry I felt like women were pushed into a certain type of expression about our personal lives and bodies and that there weren't a lot of political female poets. I used to say that I was a spoken word artist because I wanted to be Malcolm X. Now I say I do spoken word because I want to be Queen Nanny, who built the community of Jamaican Maroons. In prison activism, part of it is obviously theoretical, understanding the political systems that create prisons, and how that intersects with histories of racism and settler colonialism. But another part is about building family. I really feel that through the radio show, the Black Power Hour on Dalhousie University's campus station, we have built a family. A community of people where love and support and having a space where people can be received unconditionally is most important.

Often with activism, people will caution you not to get too caught up. Especially for academic activists, there's a sense that yes, our work can advocate, but we shouldn't lose ourselves in it. I hate that idea, that we "do research" on people but we're never of the people. When I perform poems like "Harriet Tubman," I say I feel the spirit of Harriet rise in me during the poem. People think I'm joking usually, but I genuinely feel that connection with her when I'm speaking. Prison activism is the same thing. If you don't love the people you're struggling with, I don't think that's radical struggle. Colonialism is all about cordoning off parts of ourselves, separating lived experience from knowledge, knowledge from feeling, thought from love. So fundamentally anti-colonial activism has to be based in a sense of collective experience, of shared humanity, which to me is radical love.

I'm not afraid to love through my activism. For African people, our love has always been activism, because we are not supposed to be here, and we are not supposed to love each other. One way capitalism divides Black people is through class politics and respectability. We're supposed to celebrate the Black people who "make it"—even when making it means being involved in destructive institutions that harm other Black people—and we're supposed to look down upon those of us inside prison as shameful. Too often our struggles against racism focus on advancing middle-class interests and abandoning working class people and communities. Middle-class Black people often want to capitalize off the struggle of the working class—such as referencing police shootings of working class Africans—but take no actions of real solidarity. I don't see how a Black person can be conscious in society and not be in solidarity with captive Africans under correctional control.

One of the traces prison work has left on me is just with time. Because I talk on the phone with people inside, part of me now is attuned to the different prison schedules. I'll think, "oh it's 6pm, they're locked up now." That small connection of my internal clock to the prison routine is a symbol of how once you get involved in prison activism some internal part of you recalibrates and is oriented toward the inside. In Jimmy Santiago Baca's poem, "Who Understands Me But Me," he says, "they have changed me, and I am not the same man."[3] Prisoners have changed me, and I am not the same. Radical transformation of ourselves is part of advocating for radical social change.

While I was trying to finish this paper, my friend called me from prison. He's doing life. Much of what I know about prison, from the details of dental care, to the pay scale for jobs, to the feeling of just getting a birthday card, I know from him. I meant to ask him to tell me something profound about prison that I could end this piece with, but I forgot. Instead we chatted. He just got a job and was waiting to get his boots so he could start. He asked me about my day, and told me to eat lunch. I told him I was at work and he told me he was going to the gym after work up. Then he had to go. There's nothing profound in that conversation, but that represents the daily life of activism, and a moment in the day in prison of contact with the outside. And that is how we build and sustain the struggle.

Notes

1. Frank Harris, *Oscar Wilde: His Life and Confessions*. (NY: Brentano's, 1916).

2. Eric Roach, "I Say It Was the Women," *The Flowering Rock: Collected Poems 1938-1974* (Leeds: Peepal Tree, 2012).

3. Jimmy Santiago Baca, "Who Understands Me But Me," *Immigrants in Our Own Land and Selected Early Poems* (NY: New Directions, 1990).

CHAPTER TWO

Wars on social reproduction: On feminism, the commons, and joyful militancy

An interview with Silvia Federici

SILVIA FEDERICI is a feminist activist, teacher and writer. She was a co-founder of the International Feminist Collective and the Committee for Academic Freedom in Africa. She is the author of many essays on political philosophy, feminist theory, cultural studies, and education. Her published works include: *Revolution at Point Zero: Housework, Reproduction, and Feminist Struggle*; *Caliban and the Witch: Women, the Body and Primitive Accumulation*; *A Thousand Flowers: Social Struggles Against Structural Adjustment in African Universities* (co-editor); *Enduring Western Civilization: The Construction of Western Civilization and its "Others"* (editor). She is Emerita Professor at Hofstra University (Hempstead, New York). Max Haiven interviewed Silvia in April, 2017.

MAX HAIVEN: The concept of this book is to explore how experience and struggle are related to the radical imagination. For that reason, we're beginning by asking about early and awakening formative experiences.

SILVIA FEDERICI: I have begun to speak more about my personal background and growing up in post-War Italy. Over time, it has appeared to me as more and more crucial to not only my intellectual, but also my emotional formation: my relationship to life, to capitalism, to value. The stories of the war and the memory of fascism and the war were very important; as a child, I was politicized in my family, in the everyday conversation at the dinner table. There was a continuous reconstruction of what it meant to live during fascism and the war.

MH: What sort of form did that take?

SF: The discussions were rich. My father was a teacher, but though he was anti-fascist, he never went to the hills. As I grew up, many times I asked him. "Why didn't you go up to the hills, join the partisans and fight?" His answer was that he had a family, and felt responsible towards it. But he would describe what it meant to live during that time: the Fascists would demand that teachers wear a black shirt one day a week; or they would force them to teach "fascist theory"! He would speak of his resistance, for some years, against taking the [Fascist] Party card, and then having to, because otherwise he would not have been able to continue to work. He talked about the madness of being recruited in the army and how he made himself sick, he gave himself an ulcer to be dismissed for a while. He was full of spite for Mussolini—for his speeches, his arrogant and grotesque posture, his posing as the "prince of youth," his displays as the "great man" with bare chest, going into the fields, and so on. My parents recalled their dismay at seeing his oceanic gatherings. My mother often told us about her anguish when she heard the declaration of war on the radio, and saw the squares filled with people applauding, applauding...

Then, when in 1943 Italy broke its collaboration with the Nazis and Italy became an occupied country, my mother would have to ask a Nazi commander for permission to visit her sister, a few kilometers away. And she recalled my birth (on Hitler's birthday!) with German soldiers out in the streets. She recalled the rationing of food that began in 1942. In my town, Parma, food was very much rationed during the whole period of the war. And when Mussolini came to visit, people did not protest, though the region supported the Partisans, because during his visit they lifted the rationing of food.

And then there were tons and tons of stories from my mother about the bombardments, about waking up at night and the sky was red from British or American bombs, and taking the kids (I was a few months old, my sister was two or three) and running, running, running. Each time this happened there were stories: the night my father forgot his shoes and he decided not to go back for them. If he had gone back he would have been killed because the place was totally destroyed.

I have said many times that what convinced me not to have children was my mother's stories, over and over, about waking up at night and seeing the sky red and knowing that the bombs were going to start dropping, and desperately taking her children, two little children, me included, and running and running, and then spending the night squatting in some place until it appeared to be safe. When you grow up with those stories, it's difficult to feel incentivized to want children. There was nothing coordinated, but the war itself was a very collective experience. And the generation that came out of it, the first post-war generation, all had participated in it, although we were children. Nevertheless it was a collective experience, because it had brought people together, it brought communities together. Yes, it separated them, but it also brought them together.

In that sense it was not organized; it was a silent but simultaneous decision that had many elements to it. One is the refusal of the destruction. The other is the assertion of independence as women, and later as feminists. Women came out as protagonists in the period after the war, in Italy and Germany more so than the United States. When the men were at the front, women had to confront everything at home. And many also participated actively in the resistance; many in Italy joined the partisans. I grew up with those stories too, of women partisans in the mountains, or staying home but nevertheless, helping the cause, providing infrastructure and help.

Even the women who were not openly politically involved, nevertheless, had to confront many challenges during the war. In many cases, they lived in situations where they confronted fascist militia. Italy was occupied by the Nazis after 1943, it became an enemy country, and women lived a life of struggle to procure food and to deal with all kinds of dangers. And by the end of the war it was impossible to go back to what had existed before. It's not an accident that the first generation of post-war women exploded into the feminist movement. Women began to recognize that, in order to have some independence, the first condition was to drastically reduce the number of children, and also in a broader sense take some distance from the whole path of maternity, family, and dependence on men. So there's a direct connection between, on one side, the refusal of a militarized maternity that produces soldiers for the state and, on the other, the refusal of maternity that means dependence on men, sacrifice and embracing a life where you don't have the possibility to explore your needs, your possibilities, what kind of project you want to achieve in your life.

From the beginning, Parma was one of the centres of resistance against fascism. It was the only town in Italy that opposed Mussolini's March on Rome and didn't allow the fascists to come into the town. There were three famous days of urban barricades, where the proletarians prevented the fascists from coming into their neighbourhoods. During the war, whenever the partisans would do an action, the Nazis or the fascists would retaliate by killing a lot of people, sometimes rounding up people in the street and just shooting them up. If you walk around my town, you will see that the names of the streets commemorate the people who were killed.

So I grew up in an environment where politicization was inevitable. And even as a child, I felt that the post-war period was one of intense politics because there was a question of what kind of government would emerge. The famous elections of '48 put an end to people's hope that the resistance to Fascism and to the war would actually introduce a major political change and the creation of a different kind of society, a non-exploitative society.

War's lessons: the proximity of fascism and capitalist "democracy"

MH: Looking back on that period, what sort of lessons do you think that era holds for fighting authoritarianism today? A number of people have drawn inevitable parallels between the cult of personality around Donald Trump and other neo-fascists and those around Mussolini. We seem to be entering into an age of increasing repression. What do you draw on from that moment to make sense of the present moment?

SF: It's a very important question. Especially in the 1960s, some radical social Italian movements, like *Lotta Continua,* organized and struggled primarily against what they saw as new forms of fascism. One of the great lessons that I learned growing up was that, once the war was over, much of the fascist structure remained under the United States brand of "liberation." We now know that many dozens of Nazis were allowed either to be reintegrated into post-war West Germany or to escape to Latin America, where they were able to organize. So too in Italy: most of the fascists were either reintegrated or were retired with good pensions; the fascist structures remained. The Vatican worked very closely with the United States, to, first of all, provide passports to the Nazis and the fascists who wanted to migrate to Latin America.

The post-war period in Italy was extremely repressive. The police were literally in the factories and workers known to be communists were isolated to a particular part of the plant where they would not "infect" the others. The party that came into existence and dominated Italian politics after the war was the Christian Democrats, one of the most corrupt, known to be connected with the Mafia, and having a colonial relation with the United States which always had a strong hand in Italian politics. It was said that whenever there was a big strike in Italy, the American troops would be moved from Germany to the border of Italy.

So the lesson I draw from this all is that the alternative, fascism versus democracy, is deceptive. The two work together. The experience of post-war Italy has been useful for me. It has become a litmus test for judging many developments, including the present one.

I remember when, in 1993, there was the war in Yugoslavia, and you had debates on the Left about supporting the American military intervention in order to aid the Albanian Leftists, with the idea that they would finally have an independent territory and again independence from Serbia. I used to say, "Good luck," you're deluding yourself if you think the American intervention is going to lead to you being allowed to control the new political reality in your country or have an actually independent territory. I was right. In Italy, Kosovo is called a "mafia state" because it has become the conduit for the passage of heroin from Afghanistan to Europe, with the blessing of all the NATO occupation forces. And, of course, there is also the trafficking of arms and sex workers.

Historical amnesia and imperial apologists

MH: It's a coincidence that we're talking about this only a couple of days after the United States launched a missile attack against state forces in Syria. This is really the first moment where a large section of the American ruling class media and liberal intellectuals have supported Trump, when even a few weeks ago they were calling him all sorts of very accurate names.

sf: Yes, it is an absolute turn-about! What is being fed to us is like an Indonesian shadow theatre: we only see the shadows. We need to understand what are the real forces and interests at work. American politics has always had this great capacity to muddy the water by supporting both sides, like it did with Iraq and Iran in the 1980s, to let them destroy each other and to ensure US domination of the victor and the vanquished afterwards.

mh: I think it really brings to mind the discussion you were just giving about the relationship between fascism and democracy and this sort of false dichotomy that is presented. So often, I think, here in the United States and I would also say in Canada as well, there's a sense, even on the Left, that in political discourse, you almost approve or disapprove of the action of the State, as if the State cares, and also as if they follow "our" advice. But who is this "us" that gives the advice? Something happens to the imagination when we orient it towards asking, "Well, is this imperialist action a good thing or a bad thing? What is our position? What should our state be doing?" But there's something missing about who the "we" is, and what our interests are.

sf: Moreover, there is this amnesia and this continuous refrain that "this is not what America is about." The United States has been very skillful in using its immense resources to externalize a lot of fascism that has been essential to its dominance. So you can have a democratic appearance and policies at home and then, for example, fascism in Latin America and in the areas the United States has colonized. But then there is also internal fascism; you don't have to go far at all. As you know, Jim Crow never stopped, it's just been transformed. Keeanga-Yamahtta Taylor, for instance, describes a hiatus in American politics in the past generation, with the entrance of many former Black activists into the electoral system. But generally, you don't have to go very far from the United States to see the coexistence with democratic forms of political government and very fascist regimes. This has been the history of this country, from slavery to Jim Crow to now. How can we ignore this continuity of history? Should we dismiss completely from this history the genocide of Indigenous peoples, the construction of the reservation system, that so much inspired the Nazi construction of the concentration camps, and the continuous appropriation of

Indigenous land, the continuous destruction of whatever little land they have kept in their hands?

Learning from struggles in Nigeria: debt, land, feminism, oil and study

MH: On this note of neocolonialism, I want to ask you about the influence that living and working in Nigeria has had on your thinking and activism.

SF: This was at the beginning of the Reagan period; many of us felt suffocated and the spaces that we had been able to organize in the US were shrinking. I had been involved in several feminist projects which had come to an end, or were in crisis, so the idea of spending time out of the country became very attractive. I was working in Port Harcourt, which is on the Delta of the Niger River and is the petroleum capital of Nigeria. It was an amazing time to be there: the debt crisis was beginning to hit the country. By 1974 Nigeria had been borrowing a lot of money at low interest rates, based on the high cost of oil. The international banks were pushing these loans on developing countries. Now it looks like it was a scheme to create a debt crisis, which happened in 1979, when the Federal Reserve raised interest rates. I arrived at the moment when everybody in Nigeria and in other countries were being confronted with the debt crisis. The International Monetary Fund was saying, "Take a standby loan so you can pay your creditors. But in order to get that standby loan, you have to cut wages, cut the public sector, privatize health, education," and so forth.

The first thing I saw then when I arrived was that the university was shut down by student protests and there were protests throughout society. This was an immediate introduction to the politics of the place, the politics of the student movement, the revolt of teachers. But also an introduction to the debt crisis, which I now see was the beginning of globalization and the hook that was used to re-colonize entire regions, and to turn the clock back on the anti-colonial struggle. Through debt, a whole reform process was activated that reconfigured the local political economy in a neocolonial way, shifting production towards export, forcing massive monetary devaluation, and forcing the state to disinvest in the reproduction of the local population.

My time there was also very important because I was under the impression, coming from Europe and the US, that all the land in the world had been privatized and commercialized. But I realized that, in Nigeria and throughout the rest of Africa, a lot of land was still managed through communal regimes. Clearly this "commons" had gone through many transformations throughout the colonial period; nevertheless, you still had communal forms of existence. My students and colleagues would say to me, "What? You don't have any land? You're just living on the basis of a wage? Aren't you anxious?" They were born into land; they were related to a village system they could rely on when they grew old, or if their jobs collapsed. Even in the worst case scenario they would have access to a little piece of land and a community.

So the question of land entered into my politics. When I was a politicized adolescent in Italy I always talked of workers' struggles, because there were a lot of industrial strikes. "But what about the peasants?" my mother would ask. "To you, there are only factory workers. What about your aunt who is working the land?" Only many years later did I realize that my mother had important political insights. In Nigeria, I also began to see the importance of subsistence farming in relation to reproduction. My ideas of reproductive work and the reproduction of lives and the workforce expanded from domestic work, which had been a central concern in my previous politics, to also include subsistence farming. I saw anew the working day of a woman engaged in reproductive work in Africa and Latin America also included working time in the field for subsistence. And then, if she had some excess, she would sell the produce on the side of the road, but it would be like the local market exchange. Since then, I have come to understand how crucial the land question is.

I also learned other things. First of all, student politics. I had been involved in the student movement when I came to the US in 1967, which at that time was centred on the struggle against the Vietnam war. In Nigeria I came into contact with the struggle for free education that developed in response to the disinvestment of the State in the educational sector and the removal of student allowances. Back in the US, with other people like George Caffentzis and also colleagues and students from Africa, we began to put out the *Bulletin of the Committee of Academic Freedom in Africa*, with the intent of publicizing the struggle of the African students. At the time, there was a lot of attention for the student movement in China, but none for the student movement in Africa, though people were being arrested and student unions were driven underground. We began to expose the plan of the World Bank for African education, which consisted in dismantling what had been constructed after independence. At a 1976 conference in Harare, the World Bank made it clear that, from their perspective, "Africans did not need universities." Because in their plans for the restructuring of the global economy and division of labor, Africans would be destined to be manual workers. We campaigned against it and produced a book called *A Thousand Flowers: Social Struggle against Structural Adjustment in African Universities.*

In Nigeria I also became involved with the first feminist organization in the country, "WIN" (Women in Nigeria). I collaborated with them, I went to their meetings, and contributed in a small way to the document that they prepared for the UN Nairobi Women's conferences of 1985. I couldn't go to the conference however because at that time our campus was invaded by the police. There was tear gas everywhere, students being beaten up and persecuted.

Then there were the struggles over the petroleum. In Port Harcourt, many of the teachers and students in the social sciences were involved in analyzing the effects of the petroleum exploitation. It was like being in some parts of New Jersey: the sky was always red and the delta was totally polluted. Imagine, the delta of the Niger, one of the great wonders of the world. There are thousands of very rich, fertile rivulets, full of mangrove growth. People told me that once the Delta was so rich in fish, that you could put your hand in the water and catch them. But I never ate a fish from that area. It had all been contaminated by oil drilling or the fish were scared away from the surface by the continuous lighting. Much of the environment and the crop land had been destroyed. People suffered from many diseases. They had problems with their kidneys, their eyes, and had all kinds of blood cancer.

Not surprisingly the local papers were full of stories of the people's struggle. Some complained that they had been promised money because their trees had been cut to make space for oil extraction, but it never materialized. There were struggles over spills that were never taken care of. People spoke of petroleum as a curse; the money all went to the government, it never went to them. Only a minimal part was used for public investment. Instead, people were displaced from their land, the water was contaminated, diseases proliferated. At that time, my partner, George Caffentzis, began a study of oil that became a lifetime project, though he comes from a political philosophy background. The results will be published soon in a book called *No Blood for Oil.*

During my time in Nigeria, colonialism became very real. You can read about colonialism but you have to be in a place to see it at work. This is why it was crucial for me to spend time in the former colonized world—Mexico, Latin America. These are places from which to understand where capitalism is going. I used to have the illusion that, being in the belly of the beast, in New York, you could see things clearly. That dissipated when I went to Nigeria because I saw the other side. It's impossible to understand capitalism without seeing its other sides. This is a lesson I first learned as a feminist, looking at housework: the "other" side of the factory. But there is another "other": the world of wage-less workers, the so-called peasantry who were, for a long time, invisible to the politics in the so-called industrialized countries.

Academic freedom: theirs and ours

MH: One of the things I wanted to follow up with you from that is this question about organizing for academic freedom. The type of academic freedom that you were organizing around in CAFA is very different from the academic freedom that is trumpeted from the ivory tower in North America. I'm thinking about the way that, recently, the far right and its liberal quislings in the US have seized the rhetoric of academic freedom as a way to trigger exploitable spectacles. So they'll send these neo-fascist thinkers out to universities to provoke an anti-fascist response. We end up being drawn into these very non-materialist, very reactionary debates around the abstract virtue of academic freedom and freedom of speech.

SF: Yes, absolutely. In fact, today I wouldn't use the term academic freedom. At that time we used the term because we were so much shaped by the African experience. There was a big gathering of students, intellectuals, activists, teachers in Kampala in 1990, to protest the changes that were taking place in the university. At this gathering, people provocatively used the traditionally elitist idea of academic freedom to say: academic freedom means the right to study, the right to produce knowledge outside of a commercial context. These rights were denied by the new politics of the World Bank and the IMF. So we took that up. What is academic freedom when so many people are not allowed to study because they don't have the money? We wanted to highlight those contradictions. We used the term in the provocative sense in which it was being used in Africa.

It's still important to show the contradiction because academic freedom has this aura. But the reality is that in the US as well, students are indentured servants to the banks. So how can academic freedom go hand-in-hand with liberating students from debt?

Yesterday we heard the news that the state of New York is going to eliminate some tuition fees and reintroduce open admissions for students whose families have revenues inferior to $100,000. That is good news. It's the product of a long student struggle. It does not come out of nothing. It's because students have been mobilizing in so many different ways, in New York and at the national level. It's a welcomed development and an important one, but it must be extended and expanded. I look forward to it giving fuel to student struggles.

Legacies and cycles of struggle: debt and Occupy

MH: It brings up an interesting question about how movements circulate and cycle. There was so much condemnation, of course on the right and from the liberal intelligentsia, but also from the Left, about the alleged ineffectiveness of the Occupy Movement. But one of the key demands that came out of some of the offshoots of Occupy Wall Street was precisely for free tuition, for liberation from debt. You yourself were involved in Strike Debt and other such organizations. Maybe there isn't a direct relationship where social movements arose around a single demand and the government responded. But there never is. But if we don't understand how those movements are connected to these transformations, we are left imagining that free tuition is the result of the enlightened benevolence of the ruling class.

SF: Yes! I cannot stand this pessimism and dismissal which would tell us that because movements don't achieve all that many people hoped, therefore you should dismiss even what they do achieve. Occupy politicized many youth who were going by the thousands to demonstrations; it was behind the rise of Bernie Sanders; it created all kinds of groups and struggle around the question of debt. It is student struggles that have put the question of debt on the national map. Bernie Sanders or Elizabeth Warren could only succeed and place debt on the national agenda thanks to these struggles. As George Caffentzis has often said, talk about doing something about the debt had circulated on campuses and other venues for a long time, but it was only when people, night after night, day after day, began to share their experiences that they began to realize they were all in debt, and began to think of doing something about it. Organizations like Strike Debt came out directly from the Occupy Movement, where people discovered they shared the condition of debt and also the guilt that surrounds it. The kind of exploitation you suffer when you have a debt with a bank is not the same as when you are fighting in a wage struggle where you know very clearly that you and the people around you are exploited. Debt individualizes exploitation and gives you the impression that it is your fault: you took too much money, you didn't manage it wisely, etc. Often students only confront the debt once they have left university, when they are separated from other people. So Occupy was very important because those isolated people, suffering guilt, found themselves together.

Organizing around debt is not the only movement that has come out of Occupy, people are also struggling around housing in New York. Occupy Sandy is another example where, after the 2012 hurricane, people went into neighbourhoods to organize grassroots relief and rebuilding. So I think we have to be very careful before saying: "oh, Occupy is over. Occupy did nothing." Or "it's all been corrupted," as sometimes it has been said.

Against pessimism

MH: This leads us to something that I wanted to ask you about, something that I have reflected about a lot, following your work over the years. I've also always learned a lot from the example that you've set of a kind of critical optimism. I've noticed two things: one of them is that you've steadfastly refused to take a pessimistic view of social movements and instead tried to see them and theorize the present conjecture in a way that works and builds along with them, and that builds a sense of history. Second, in your work, while you have never failed to criticize other thinkers very directly when necessary, it is never your focus; your focus is always on generating something new and radicalizing. And so I wanted to ask you about how you live a life of a radical intellectual with a sense of optimism, with a sense of purpose, with a sense of solidarity, when so much about the intellectual production on the

Left, and especially when it is tied to academe, seems to promote a much more negative approach.

sf: Yes, I cannot stand the kind of competitiveness and the kind of dismissal of other people's ideas and self-promotion that at times infiltrates radical politics, particularly when connected with the academic experience. I think we should stay away from that, as much as possible, even when it comes to people we disagree with. I always try to see what a positive contribution would be. I criticize certain things, but I really want to focus on what we can learn, and also recognize people's work. In terms of optimism, I think it is a duty; not optimism in the sense of expecting things to always be good, but in the sense of expecting that things can be done. And expecting that, yes, even in very negative situations, such as we find ourselves in today, there is something that can be done.

I say that for two reasons. First, because pessimism is useless. You might as well be defeated. There's now a slogan that goes around that says "the struggle that is most defeated is the one in which you never engage." So if you assume that things are so bad that nothing can be done, well, that's already embracing a defeat. Second: For all the backbiting and competitiveness, I'm always impressed with the beauty of social movements and the great number of people who are giving so much to the struggles. And the more the years go by, the more I am impressed about how many beautiful people I meet. This gives me enormous joy and an enormous sense of life. Even if it's tiring, and doing a lot of things is tiring, it gives me a lot of energy, and a lot of hope in the future.

These days I always say that the reason why there is so much violence by the Trumps and the Clintons of this world, why states have to use all their methods to terrorize us with weapons, wars, and imprisonments, is because they see in front of them an immense resistance: a world of millions of people who, if they were not completely depressed, repressed, displaced, terrorized, would be actively engaged. And nevertheless they are!

How many people are really committed to live in a world where there is such justice, where there is no hierarchy, where there is no exploitation, where there is no warfare, where there are no jails? For all the people that we see that are committed to a very competitive and destructive system, there are many more who want a different world. They're active, and there's an immense amount of generosity. It's very important, politically, that we keep our eyes focused on that, and that we see that this is what *they*, those in power, also see.

Joyful militancy and radical generosity

SF: I gave an interview some time ago in which I spoke about joyful militancy. It doesn't mean that, doing political work, you don't suffer, but suffering is not self-sacrificing. It is very dangerous to approach political work as if it is alienated labour. If you say "Oh, my God, I have to go to another meeting" or "Oh, my God, I have to write another pamphlet" you must stop and review what you are doing. We struggle and try to change things because we are unhappy, because we don't like this society, because we need to improve our lives. It's not sacrifice. Struggle is supposed to make you grow, struggle is supposed to heal your pain, to socialize your pain: you are together with other people who are suffering with you. Now you can begin to creatively respond to this suffering, and that's where the joyfulness of militancy comes in. Politics has to be a healing process, a process of creative growth.

There is also the importance of being generous with people, particularly with younger people, and not assuming right away that what they say is exactly what they think, or that what they think cannot change tomorrow. I realized over the years that people live with so much fear in their bones, even if we are not aware of it; this society makes us very fearful. So there are certain automatic responses that we have, especially when we are young and may not have had a lot of experience. When posed with a question or challenge you feel you need to respond, even if you are not sure. So you reach for something that is safe, that makes you look like you know something, like you have something to say. So many times, people in meetings rehearse things they have heard but not necessarily processed. It is not something coming from a deep experience, from a commitment; it can be very superficial. They are instinctively cautious because there is this generalized sense that mistakes can have very, very serious consequences. So, one has to be very careful to not immediately assume a person is right-wing or doesn't understand anything. It comes from this systematic, strategic antagonism: always feeling that it is imperative to be antagonistic. So I think a certain generosity is vital. It's very important to hold on to the possibility for all kinds of change and to see that people might say one thing today and go on to have other experiences that will transform them.

I think we speak a lot of the collapse of civility in social interactions under neoliberalism. I think that we need to respond by constructing civility in our movements. Generosity with others is very important.

CHAPTER THREE

Sticking around in struggle: Lessons from and for the long haul

Chris Dixon

CHRIS DIXON, originally from Alaska, is a longtime anarchist organizer, writer, and educator. He serves on the board of the Institute for Anarchist Studies and the advisory board for the activist journal *Upping the Anti*. Dixon lives in Ottawa, on unceded and unsurrendered Algonquin territory, where he is a member of the Punch Up Collective. His most recent book is *Another Politics: Talking Across Today's Transformative Movements*, published by University of California Press. Find him at WritingWithMovements.com.

How will we stay involved for the long haul? This is a question I've heard a lot over the last decade as I've travelled around North America talking with people involved in a variety of radical movements. It came up in conversations with community organizers in Boston, Indigenous solidarity activists in Winnipeg, labour organizers in Los Angeles, and youth activists in Vancouver, among other places. It clearly resonates, particularly in this period when so many people are thinking about what it will take to fight for and win a better world.

The basic idea of the long haul is that building large-scale movements capable of fundamentally transforming society will require people to work together, with persistence, over decades and across generations. Those of us committed to creating radical change can and should fight for victories along the way, and as the late historian Howard Zinn regularly said, we can anticipate that there will be many unexpected turns, both positive and negative.[1] But we will have to persevere with few certainties, many setbacks, and no infallible formulas for action. Although not easy, the only way forward is to stick around in struggle.

Based on this conviction, I began giving short presentations called "For the Long Haul" while on tour in 2014-2015 with my book *Another Politics*. Very consistently, these presentations catalyzed discussions among engaged—and often surprisingly multi-generational—groups of activists. People raised important questions and offered valuable insights. In what follows, I'd like to share a little about my own pathway into these discussions and amplify the collective brilliance I've come across. Some of the quotes I share here are from formal interviews I conducted and others are from discussions at presentations and workshops, including from people whose names I unfortunately don't know.

A long view

The notion of the long haul was central to how I came into radical politics. I grew up as a white guy in a middle-class suburb of Anchorage, Alaska, on traditional Dena'ina territory. My relatively privileged life didn't offer me many resources for making sense of the colonialism, poverty, gendered violence, militarism, and ecological destruction that I encountered in Alaska. But while attending a public alternative school in the early 1990s, I was lucky to have anarchist and socialist teachers who presented more critical ways of understanding the world. As the US government was carrying out the first Gulf War, my friends and I were taking classes in Third World studies, the civil rights movement, and women's literature. We read radical history and theory voraciously, discussed politics constantly, and started organizing around environmentalism, feminism, labour solidarity, and democracy at our school.

We also began to see ourselves as participants in long lineages of struggle for justice and dignity. While learning about past movements was an important part of this for me, even more crucial was building relationships with elder radicals who had been active in those movements. One of these people was Ruth Sheridan, whom I first met when she came to speak in a labour history class I was taking in eighth grade. Sheridan, then in her seventies (and now in her nineties), is a lifelong anarchist who has participated in the Industrial Workers of the World, the women's liberation movement, the Central American solidarity movement, waves of anti-war organizing, and much more. She has a keen mind, a hearty laugh, an indomitable spirit, and a fierce love for people.

As I came to know Sheridan and other older radicals in her circle, I started to gain some perspective. None of these people were famous; their names will probably never appear in history books and their individual contributions will be mostly forgotten, except by their close comrades and loved ones. They knew this, and yet they kept going, sustaining lives in struggle through major wars, mass movements, state repression, political transitions, new upsurges, and crushing defeats. They were in for the long haul; they carried, as Spanish anarchists used to say, a new world in their hearts. Their steadfastness profoundly shaped my political consciousness.

One of the most important things I learned from Sheridan and others like her is that sticking around in struggle is easier when we cultivate "a long view." I understand this expression to mean two things. One is a deeply-felt sense that things have been—and can be—otherwise. After all, most of the social relations and structures that we currently take for granted—race, prisons, the nuclear family, waged work, fossil fuels, and much more—are comparatively recent developments in human history; they can be challenged and changed. Second, as a migrant justice activist from Tucson pointed out to me, a long view involves viscerally experiencing ourselves as links in an intergenerational chain of struggle; we build on the sacrifices and contributions of those who came before us, and we make our own sacrifices and contributions for those who will come next. With this kind of long view, we can understand (and, just as important, evaluate) our efforts through not only what they accomplish now, but also the groundwork they lay for the future.

Challenges: Replicating oppression and taking a paranoid stance

But let's be honest: holding a long view is helpful but not sufficient for staying involved for the long haul. In fact, there are very consistent challenges we face in sustaining movements, and these challenges are substantially shaped by how power is presently organized and administered. The ruling relations in this society generate immense wealth and power for a very small number of people while creating differentiated misery among the vast majority and ecological destruction across the planet. Some challenges we confront in building resilient movements—such as precarious work, fragmented communities, state violence, and people being pushed out of their homes—are direct results of this social structure. Overcoming these sorts of challenges will require organizing and struggle on a scale that most of us are really only beginning to imagine.

Other challenges for sustaining long-haul efforts are more directly rooted in movements, specifically movement cultures. These are ways in which we, as activists and organizers, trip ourselves up through our habitual patterns. While these kinds of challenges grow out of ruling relations, those of us involved in movements bear real responsibilities for sustaining them. I'll focus on two such challenges here, both of which have come up regularly in my discussions with people across the US and Canadian contexts.

The first is the tendency for movements, usually unconsciously, to replicate oppressive values and practices from the society in which we live. This is nothing new; many who have come before us (notably, radical women of colour feminists in the 1960s and 1970s) have observed this tendency. Still, it's worth repeating the insight: even as we fight hierarchies based on gender, ability, race, sexuality, class, and other ruling relations, these hierarchies have shaped us and we frequently participate in reproducing them. As New York prison industrial complex abolitionist Pilar Maschi said to me, "We're trying to break down the system, and it lies in all of us."

We can see many examples of this: the types of people (often men, usually white and non-disabled, frequently university-educated) who most often step confidently into leadership roles in movements, the ongoing reality of sexual assault among activists, and the movement activities (such as writing, public speaking, and high-risk direct action) that regularly get the most social recognition. This is also visible in the exclusionary assumptions that sometimes get built into campaigns, as for instance, when immigrant rights efforts have used the slogan "we're not criminals," which leaves behind anyone who has ever been entangled with the criminal justice system.

This is a significant challenge. Oppressive values and practices don't just mar our liberatory aspirations. They also undermine our effectiveness: they spread hurt and distrust, corrode alliance-building, impede visionary strategy-making, damage and sometimes destroy organizations, and hold people back from stepping into their full capabilities. And though I understand why many radicals have become jaded about all of this, I side with those who say we can do better.

A key part of this is recognizing that no one is untouched by power relations. As feminist theorist and activist Alexis Shotwell argues:

> What's needed, instead of a pretense to purity that is impossible in the actually existing world, is something else. We need to shape better practices of responsibility and memory for our placement in relation to the past, our implication in the present, and our potential creation of different futures.[2]

This means working, with commitment and intention, to shift oppressive values and practices—and reduce their everyday harms—without pretending to be untainted by them. It means that, even with the best of intentions, our efforts will be imperfect and contradictory. Building long-haul movements, I believe, requires patience, humility, and a determination to struggle with this challenge without easy answers or quick resolution.

The second challenge is the tendency toward suspicion, rivalry, and dismissal in activist circles. A long-time radical at an event in Boston described this as "a climate of contempt on the Left." And though rarely written about, this is something many have experienced. Indeed, whenever this topic comes up in discussions, I've found it quickly evokes head nods and horror stories about takedowns on social media, organizational territorialism, activist social status hierarchies, sectarian posturing, and a general atmosphere of radical self-righteousness.

Kim Smith and Nick Montgomery, two graduate student activists I met in Victoria, helped me to better understand this tendency. Drawing on a concept from the queer theorist Eve Sedgwick, they propose that "paranoid reading" has become the dominant mode of engagement on the radical Left.[3] This is a way of relating with people, ideas, and activities by looking primarily for their failures and limitations; it's about criticizing first and, if at all, asking questions later. Smith and Montgomery suggest that "a paranoid stance tends towards constant vigilance, so that there can be no bad surprises. But the upshot of this is that there can't be any surprises at all when we're paranoid, because we close off our capacity to be curious, open, and vulnerable." This stance, they clarify, is justified and useful at times. However, when it's a dominant approach, "it tends to force out other ways of relating.

Kindness, curiosity, gratitude, and other ways of relating can come to seem naïve or counter-productive when paranoia is the reflex." There are some clear reasons why this is such a widespread tendency. Ways of relating based on objectification, competition, and exclusion are deeply ingrained in how power works in this society; they're crucial for sustaining structural hierarchies with life-and-death consequences. So, it's not surprising that these corrosive ways of relating seep into movements and that they've thrived in the last few decades of weakness and defeat for the Left. In this period when radical activist culture has become closely connected to universities, it's also not surprising that "paranoid reading," as a pervasive mode in academia, has had such influence on the Left.

Still, I'm convinced that we have a responsibility to reach toward other, more affirmative, ways of being and acting. As Montreal anti-prison organizer Helen Hudson pointed out to me, "struggle can be a really humanizing experience." That is, when people come together to fight collectively, we can feel our own humanity and the humanity of others in profound ways. People are more likely to stick around, I believe, when movements offer opportunities to experience kindness, curiosity, gratitude, and care as part of effective collective action to change the world.

Lessons: Developing organizations and organizing intergenerationally

Beyond working through challenges, there are also tangible things we can do right now to build long-haul movements. This has become more clear to me as I have spent time talking with experienced organizers and learning from longer-lasting radical efforts. Across North America, there are thousands of people who are deeply, earnestly engaged in transformative initiatives and who are developing valuable knowledge about what they're doing. Facing many similar difficulties, activists and organizers are crafting a variety of innovative approaches for sustaining struggles. Unfortunately, though, we frequently lack the time and mechanisms for sharing what we're learning across places and movements. Here, in one small effort to remedy this, I'll highlight two lessons that I've encountered repeatedly.

The first is that long-haul movements need organizations—intentionally structured groups of people with shared goals and activities. This is something I've heard from many people, but someone who makes this point particularly well is Rachel Herzing, an Oakland-based prison industrial complex abolitionist and founding member of Critical Resistance. During a conversation with me in Berkeley, Herzing said, "Re-orienting toward organization and talking about the variety of formations it can take—whether that's a network, an organization, a coalition, etc.— really is important to me in terms of thinking about the long term. So, what is possible to build not only as a collection of individuals but when you put an organizational form to work in terms of organizing?" Part of what I take from this is that organizations, at their best, can become much more than "collections of individuals": they can generate collective power and steadily build, even during movement downturns. Crucially, organizations can also maintain a long view, holding memory while developing strategy.

I recognize that this point may be controversial. In some parts of the anti-authoritarian Left especially, I've encountered reticence towards developing anything more than small and/or short-term groups and projects. I have some sympathy for this. Too often on the Left "building organizations" actually means erecting party or party-like structures that tend to be top-down, male-dominated, obsessed with a "political line," instrumental in how they treat people, and vanguardist in how they relate with popular struggles. But with care and intention, I think we can avoid that long-standing rut. As Herzing suggested, let's explore a variety of forms. If we want to grow and coordinate long-haul movements, we need resilient, bottom-up organizations through which people can, together, develop liberatory visions, make plans, take action, learn, be accountable, and care for and defend one another.

Thankfully, activists and organizers are already engaged in some valuable organizational experiments. These include multi-tendency Left organizations such as Solidarity Halifax, grassroots coalitional efforts such as the Southern Movement Assemblies in the US South, radical worker centres such as Montreal's Immigrant Workers Centre, collectively-run nonprofits such as the Sylvia Rivera Law Project in New York City, democratic membership organizations such as the Coalition of Immokalee Workers in South Florida, networks of movement-based collectives such as No One Is Illegal in the Canadian context, working-class self-defense organizations such as the Seattle Solidarity Network, and bottom-up labour unions such as the Chicago Teachers Union. We can learn a lot from the experiences of all of these models while we also experiment further.

The second lesson is that long-haul movements have to be intergenerational. Sustained efforts to transform the world need contributions and continuity from people throughout their lives. One person who has consistently articulated this point is Rahula Janowski, an anti-racist organizer with the Catalyst Project in San Francisco. In a 2007 article for *Left Turn*, she laid it out very clearly: "mono-generational movements that do not include people in all stages of life will neither move nor win. We need communities that are strong, that can withstand difficult times and challenges, and that can nurture and support their members to continue the work. A community of resistance that is multi-generational will have a continuum of memory, will carry lessons from one generation to the next, and will be a base for strong multi-generational movements."[4]

We still have a long way to go before we have movement cultures in which most people stick around as they grow older and, particularly, as they have children. In radical activist scenes especially, people tend to "age out" by their thirties, if not earlier. But lately I've been excited to encounter more and more people who are serious about intergenerational movement-building. Doing this well, they suggest, will require growing in at least a couple of directions.

One is about opening space for kids and families. It's no coincidence that some of most influential advocates for intergenerational movements (including Victoria Law, China Martens, Cynthia Oka, and others) are mothers. They bring sharp perspectives about the ways in which many radical initiatives, mostly unintentionally, exclude children and the adults responsible for them. They also highlight the benefits of welcoming families in movement efforts: more intentionality around caregiving activities, deepened relationship-building, new opportunities for organizing, more play and creativity, and greater participation and leadership from the women and gender nonconforming people who overwhelmingly tend to care for kids.

Some of the most tangible efforts to take up this direction of work are city-based radical childcare collectives, many of which loosely coordinate through the Intergalactic Conspiracy of Childcare Collectives. Closely collaborating with grassroots organizations, these collectives provide childcare for parents involved in political activities while developing broader kid-friendly movement culture. Such efforts offer much to build on.

Another direction for intergenerational growth is opening space for people beyond their early adulthoods and especially in their later years. One thing that has repeatedly struck me as I've traveled is how much younger and older radicals, particularly in bigger cities, rarely interact. (And bear in mind that, in youth-oriented activist time, "older" can be as little as five years' age difference.) This kind of generational segregation is tremendously debilitating for movements. It deprives older people of the energy and insight of younger people, and it cuts younger people off from the endurance and knowledge of older people.

What can we do to change this? Building organizations, as I mentioned earlier, is key. We could really use more structures that hold and nourish people as they age, encounter new life demands, and continue to stay involved in political activities. Disability justice also offers a crucial starting point for building intergenerational movements. As organizers in numerous places have told me, this partly means creating organizations and campaigns with multiple points of entry and engagement, rather than simplistically assuming that people are either available for everything at any time or are not serious activists. Across life stages and abilities, people experience a variety of limits on what—and how much—they can do, and they also have a beautifully wide array of contributions to make. We just need the structures and culture to recognize, invite, and facilitate them.

We can also learn from activists and organizers who have already been cultivating cross-generational relationships. In Vancouver, for instance, No One Is Illegal has been conducting and filming interviews with older radicals and making the videos available through its Inheriting Resistance project. I've found that people involved in supporting political prisoners tend to be especially deliberate about this kind of relationship building. They understand that many dedicated revolutionaries of earlier generations have been imprisoned or murdered, and thus are significantly cut off from younger generations. In the words of Helen Hudson, "the state actively tries to separate generations of organizers." This analysis is partly what led Hudson and others to work on the Certain Days: Freedom for Political Prisoners Calendar, a yearly cross-generational collaborative project between younger activists and older imprisoned radicals. These types of initiatives point toward the vibrant intergenerational movements that, with intentionality and creativity, we can grow.

Building in a movement moment

We are in a profoundly uncertain moment. While the election of Donald Trump has revealed power relations and antagonisms that have long been in motion, it's horrifyingly clear that those who rule are now accelerating a program of social immiseration and ecological devastation. I write these words only a few short weeks into the Trump government, and I have learned quickly that making any political predictions is, at best, unhelpful.

But it does seem as if something big is breaking open. Millions of people, not only in the US context but around the world, have taken action in response to the Trump government. They've been marching, occupying airports, donating huge amounts of money to dissident organizations, fighting proto-fascists in the streets, holding emergency community meetings, pressuring elected officials, mounting legal campaigns, setting up community defense networks, blockading corporate and government offices, and resisting in other ways that we may never know about. All of this activity is full of tensions and contradictions, as is always the case when people who mostly haven't participated in collective action before start mobilizing in big numbers.

For all of the uncertainty, then, this also feels like a movement moment. It has for several years now, actually. In the US context, the Movement for Black Lives has blossomed alongside a growing movement against the prison industrial complex, the fight against the Dakota Access Pipeline has illuminated a wide arena of anti-colonial struggle, and there are still significant reverberations from the Occupy movement experience. In the Canadian context, Idle No More has energized a new generation of Indigenous people, and the Quebec student movement has set a benchmark for large-scale, combative struggles against austerity. Across the continent, migrant justice and climate justice organizing are especially on the rise, and activists involved in both are increasingly bringing direct action and radical vision. And there is much more happening too. Although movements still are quite weak, these are encouraging openings.

Steph Guilloud, an organizer with Project South in Atlanta, summed this up well during a discussion in Brooklyn: "so many people are moving into motion right now." Consequently, she said, "a big question that faces longtime organizers is how do we support large numbers of people moving into motion and sustain that activation over time?" At least in part, this is a question of the long haul: how do we develop movement cultures and structures that can last beyond the high points of mobilizations, maintain momentum, and provide ways for people to stay involved in lifelong struggle? We can answer this by reckoning with challenges and limitations, especially ones we generate ourselves, and building on the rich experiences and insights that our movements possess. This, I believe, is how we can turn a moment of upsurge into a sustained confrontation with dominant institutions and relations, and realize the new world in so many hearts.

Notes

1. Howard Zinn, *The Zinn Reader: Writings on Disobedience and Democracy* (New York: Seven Stories Press, 1997), 639.

2. Alexis Shotwell, *Against Purity: Living Ethically in Compromised Times* (Minneapolis: University of Minnesota Press, 2016), 7-8.

3. Eve Sedgwick, *Touching Feeling: Affect, Pedagogy, Performativity* (Durham: Duke University Press, 2003), 123-153.

4. Rahula Janowski, "Collective Parenting for Collective Liberation," *Left Turn*, February 2007.

CHAPTER FOUR

No future without us:
Capitalist patriarchy and the struggle to liberate mothering

Halifax Motherhood Collective
Candida Hadley, Susanne Marshall, and Andrea Smith

CANDIDA HADLEY is an acquisitions and development editor with Fernwood Publishing. She is also a feminist activist and a mother of two. She lives on the unceded and unsurrendered Mi'kmaw territory of Kjipuktuk (Halifax, Nova Scotia).

SUSANNE MARSHALL is an academic editor and the publications manager for Dalhousie Architectural Press. Her research investigates globalization, mass culture, and the politics of regional identity in Canada; she has taught Canadian literature at Saint Mary's University, Dalhousie University and Mount Saint Vincent University. She has two young children.

ANDREA SMITH works as a health researcher and is a PhD dropout. She was futher politicized by her experience of mothering her young child and helped found the Halifax Motherhood Collective as a response.

As feminists, we have a habit of understanding the political nature of our personal experiences—that our experiences, far from being individualized and unique are rather bound together by the broader economic and social relations in which we live. And so when we had children, we again turned to understand how the invisibility of mothering was linked to patriarchy and capitalism. And so it was that we came together to form the Halifax Motherhood Collective and try to bring the politics of motherhood into the light.

The three of us came together to form the Halifax Motherhood Collective when our children were young. Each of us was bound in the isolation that seems to have become the norm for many first time mothers in English-speaking Canada and beyond, struggling to make personal and political sense of the new experiences and roles into which we were now being thrust. Upon coming together, we decided to hold an alternative Mother's Day event to draw attention to the politics of the experiences and the ideals of motherhood, broadly conceived. The event was well attended, and, interestingly, included few of the "usual suspects" of the Left. The people who joined us generously shared their stories of isolation, loneliness, pressures, and a lack of support and community. We heard from single mothers, co-parenting mothers, queer mothers, women of colour, stay-at-home mothers, and working-outside-the-home mothers (as well as some fathers and allies) and though their stories differed in the details, the same themes ran through everyone's story. We had planned to spend the first half of the session sharing our personal stories and the second addressing how to intervene and effect change. But we never got to the second part; the need to talk about the isolation and the social pressure of parenting—to be part of a community, even momentarily—was palpable and urgent. How did we get to this point? How did this work—this work of care for the people around us, this work which is often the most meaningful and fulfilling work that humans do—become so devalued, unappreciated, and invisible?

The answers, we argue, are found at the intersection of patriarchy and capitalism. In our political work, we try to understand the connections between our personal experiences of motherhood and the broader systems of exploitation and oppression in which we live. We recognize that our description of motherhood and our organizing is located and comes from our particular place—we are three white, well-educated women living in Atlantic Canada. But many women find themselves entangled in more complex intersections—where oppression based on race, sexuality and ability, for example, further complicate their experiences of mothering. Where Indigenous women must perform motherhood to the dictates of their colonial oppressor and still risk having their children taken away; where Black mothers have to teach their kids to fear the police so they do not get shot; where poor mothers can barely see their children because they have to work three jobs to put food on the table. We make no claim that our description and analysis of motherhood is universal, complete, or even in some cases adequate. Yet it is our intention that by grounding our politics in the social economic relations of North America—patriarchal capitalism—we can find shared ground upon which all mothers— for every configuration of motherhood—exist and struggle.

Shaping our thinking and our process

CH: My story always seems to begin with Fred. One day, when I was eight years old, I asked my mother what we were having for dinner. "Fred" was her answer. I don't think I had any particular affection for the rooster who strutted so proudly around our yard guarding his harem of hens, but it was perhaps the first time I understood where meat came from. I politely declined to eat Fred that night.

I finally dived into vegetarianism—and animal rights activism—in high school. But it was in university that I began to walk the path towards radical politics. I read a book about the conflict between the Cree and the animal rights movement, and for the first time I was challenged to think differently about my animal rights agenda; to understand it within a broader political context. It was here that I began to learn about systemic and structural inequality, and the intersection of inequalities. I moved on from my single-issue struggles to learn about capitalism, racism, patriarchy—to understand that this is about a system that ensures the perpetuation of injustice. Barbara Ehrenreich, Maria Mies, and Silvia Federici were powerful influences on my understanding of capitalism and the devaluation of women and reproductive labour.

Becoming a mother, in a new town with no family and few friends, was one of the most difficult experiences of my life. I knew nothing about taking care of a baby. I am fortunate to have a partner who lives his politics and participated equally in our reproductive labour, but despite co-parenting, and all of the sacrifices my partner made to be an active and engaged father, it was an incredibly difficult year. I was isolated, lonely, and scared.

I want something better for mothers—and for everyone engaged in care work. This is the most valuable and most rewarding work there is. We deserve better than isolation and loneliness.

sm: When I was seven years old my grandfather, a small-town banker, gave my brother an heirloom, a hundred-dollar gold coin, because my brother was a boy. It was startling being confronted with the basic value that maleness has in our society. I was furious—and I became a feminist. I came of age in the time of the Montreal massacre. Later, training as an academic, I embraced theorizations of gender and society that challenged norms for women. I joined campus feminist groups and created radio series. But my sense of who I was and how the world worked shifted abruptly when I became a mother. Despite a supportive partner and family in my home city, my first months at home, alone with a newborn, were existentially disorienting and difficult on a practical level. I knew very few people with children. Those I knew were all working outside the home. Community supports were rare, hard to travel to, and not really meant for someone in my comparatively privileged circumstances. I looked at my world with new eyes, as do countless parents. What I saw was a world that exists for individuals pursuing extremely individualized lives planned to the inch: lives that value and revolve around the pursuit of wealth and isolated achievement. I was suddenly living a life with new definitions and goals, a life focused on another human being, with new and very physical demands and hardships.

I met Andrea and Candida. Sharing similar analytical backgrounds, we assessed the strangeness of our lives as mothers. I read bits of French feminist thinker Elisabeth Badinter and American commentator Judith Warner amidst nursing and numbing sleeplessness. We decided our own conversations needed to go further, to reach out to others and bring more attention to the social constructions that variously fetishize, regulate, and devalue motherhood, parenting, and children in our society. I'm not a natural organizer, and I feel like a newcomer in many ways, but I feel strongly that this is important work.

as: Punk rock was instrumental in my political education. As an anarchofeminist in the 90s, my consciousness was shaped by violence against women, including the date rape campaigns of the day. I was drawn to the fight for women's autonomy over our bodies and the ways in which living in a patriarchal society means that girls and women are sexualized and subjected to violence and control. Politically, this lead to campaigns around women's health, including defending abortion rights and to a lesser extent, about medicalization of pregnancy and birth. My anti-state politics coincided with these struggles in trying to keep the state out of women's reproductive lives.

While my own fertility misadventures gave new fuel for my analysis of the politics of reproduction, nothing has politically transformed me like having a child. I, like so many first time mothers, found myself in a completely different universe, in a profound isolation that I still struggle to understand. But it was then that I was hit, emotionally and analytically, by how women's unwaged reproductive labour is the very stuff that keeps society going. It is the stuff of life, the activities that give meaning to our existence, on a day-to-day basis, through our connection to other beings. It is how we meet our human needs—emotional, physical, psychological—by caring and being cared for by others. It's supporting people through struggle and hard times, which ever increasingly seem to fall upon us, even in the privileged spaces in Canada. So it is necessary for our human form of life. The centrality of these politics to life itself offers me, in earnest, a sense of possibility, of hope, something to fight for, not just against.

Reflecting on social reproduction and social change

We approach our collective work from the perspective that patriarchy is manifested in political and economic relations and in ideology, and that it oppresses and exploits women's knowledge and labour. It is foundational to the development and continuation of capitalism. Patriarchy allows for the devaluation of women's contribution to society, and capitalism borrows this devaluation of women for its own benefit. Our understanding of this relationship emerges from the work of some amazing Marxist feminists such as Silvia Federici and Maria Mies, who have done extensive research into the history of reproductive labour. From them we understand that the distinction between reproductive and productive labour is not merely a "natural" phenomenon emerging from the evolutionary development of human nature, rather it is a social construct developed very deliberately in order to birth and sustain capitalism.

Through an exploration of the historical literature of Europe, Silvia Federici traces the development of the conception of housework and the private sphere, and women's relegation to it, and finds that these notions actually emerge in the 16th century with the beginnings of capitalism. At this time capitalism created a previously unknown distinction between reproductive and productive work, defining two separate realms, and over the course of the 16th and 17th centuries pushed women into the unremunerated reproductive realm. It did this through a number of means: by expelling women from the productive workforce, and then from the guilds, or worker collectives, and then by denying a wage to reproductive work. Capitalism also enclosed the commons, those shared lands and resources on which autonomous communities depended.

The destruction of the commons—the shared knowledge, skills, and resources humans require to live—is vital to the ideology and material relations of capitalism. It was only through this process that capitalism gave rise to private property relations, and the idea of private ownership of land and productive capacity. As capitalism expands and parcels all facets of life into commodities to be exchanged, it has reshaped social relations. Increasingly, human needs are only able to be met through commodity exchange, as peoples' abilities to meet their own needs without relying on capital are largely undermined and destroyed. In North America, this has reinforced an individualistic and atomized view of social relations, perhaps best exemplified by the idea of the nuclear family. Our experience in the Anglophone North today is one of decreasing collective care and increasing privatization. Too often it has become the responsibility of the individual to care for themselves and their loved ones.

As capitalism grew, new conceptions of human nature also emerged. Masculine scientific approaches took for granted a competitive, selfish and greedy vision of the world, which would be articulated in the theories of evolution that advocated the survival of the fittest. Born is the anachronistic image of man-the-hunter and women-the-gatherer, where the division of labour is naturalized. These narratives about human nature, where progress, growth and the individual reign supreme, are deployed purposefully in support of the division of gender roles to further the development of capitalism. Capitalism rewrites our stories to construct a reality that serves its own ends.

The devaluation of mothering and children under capitalist patriarchy

While the marketing of motherhood paints an idyllic picture of white economically mobile women jogging with their strollers through parks smiling in the sunshine, many women's (and even theirs) lived experience of mothering is not so rosy. For many women, particularly women who do not fit so neatly into the white, middle class, heteronormative mould, mothering is undervalued and trivialized. We argue that mothering is undervalued so that that reproductive labour—the day-to-day unwaged work of growing, raising, and supporting children and families—can be exploited. By exploiting reproductive labour capitalism produces workers and consumers with minimal investment. When the work of reproducing society that is childcare, elder care, and health care is downloaded onto women, the state is released from the responsibility to care for its citizens, and capital is released from the responsibility to pay for it. Where the state does maintain some responsibility for care, it undervalues that work and those who do it to such an extent that the costs no longer have any correspondence to its importance and its necessity to society's functioning. Capitalism relies on the exploitation of human labour and nature to build its profits, and the exploitation of women's reproductive labour is extremely lucrative. That is why it is essential to think about reproduction not in terms of biology but more broadly, in terms of perpetuating and sustaining human life. Many assume mothers should do this work out of love for their children, or that it is a choice to have children, and hence does not require compensation. But love does not put food on the table. Under a capitalist system, where money is paramount, if we are not paid for our reproductive labour, then we—and by extension our children—must sell our labour elsewhere. This situation results in the dual exploitation of women's labour today as both waged and non-waged workers.

While the devaluation of reproductive and caring labour is central to women's experiences of mothering, we argue that there is another aspect of parenting in the Anglophone North Atlantic that is equally problematic: the devaluation of children.

Ideas and norms about childhood and the place of children in society is an ever-changing issue within and across societies and across time. But in our current context children are somehow less than human—or perhaps more accurately, not *yet* human. Within capitalism, they are not yet productive workers or consumers (though this is changing) and so they are not actually of value. As such, we don't have to respect or interact with them as independent human beings—and can ignore their thoughts, needs, wants, and values. They're just dirty, loud, messy, tantrum-throwing inconveniences.

Contrarily, too, this sense of proto-humanness, of the child as a blank slate who will become human, advances the rhetorical use of children as perfect ideals, separated from the failures, preferences, and partialities of adult subjecthood. For example, we talk about "child" poverty to focus upon the blameless child, while often unfairly blaming the parents for the circumstances of their poverty.

There is the old adage attributed to the British aristocracy that children should be seen and not heard, but we would argue that, in our current context, children are expected to be neither seen nor heard, at least outside of the particular child-designated spaces in which they are welcome: school, park, indoor play space, children's floor of the library—essentially, in spaces that are designed specifically for children. But when it comes to spaces that are allegedly designed for everyone, they are often not welcome.

Hostility towards, and even occasional outright discrimination against children is widespread and largely acceptable. Even from our place of privilege we have experienced strangers executing violence against our children, have been made to feel unwelcomed in public spaces, knowing full well that these types of experiences are even more pronounced outside of our relative bubble of privilege. Perhaps more mundane, some people—often responding to romanticised notions of having children and the nuclear family—happily declare themselves child-free, as if a lack of children in one's life is an accomplishment or an act of rebellion against capitalist conformity. Such hostility and discrimination are made possible and acceptable—as it so often is when we Other certain groups of people—because children are not considered fully human.

This capitalist notion of children as the property, even the whim, of their parents, this removal of children from the public sphere, affects our sense of what is reasonable and right in our private lives, in public spaces, and in our working lives as well, whether we are parents or not. An example of this can be found in the workplace where we see discussion about allowing parents more flexibility in choosing their hours, and priority for shifts that accommodate their care work, such as permitting parents to opt out of night or weekend shifts. The common backlash is very telling. Without suggesting that this should not be a contentious issue, it says a great deal about the value we place on reproductive labour and children. One might rebut that they also want to have private time to "hang out" with their family, for example. But parents are not requesting flexibility in their work because they want to "hang out" with their kids. In our system of privatized and individualized care, parents require time to spend with their kids because it is their responsibility to care for them, to keep them alive, and teach them how to function in this world.

Understanding the work of parenting as "hanging out" reinforces the devaluation of reproductive work. It is no longer work, but becomes a leisure activity that you chose to take on. And if the activity is not work, then it does not have any economic value, and need not be compensated for. But it is work. And it is work that is essential to humanity. Under capitalism, this work is exploited to further the relations of wage labour, but care work is arguably the most important work of all and we should all feel an obligation to engage in some form of reproductive or caring work. Being free from the exhausting, time-consuming—but also deeply meaningful—work of care should not be a badge of honour, rather, it is our collective responsibility to care for each other.

The work of mothering (and parenting, and caring more broadly) is undervalued because it is configured as women's work, because it is separated from and discounted relative to productive work, and because it involves the care of people who are themselves undervalued and supposedly non-productive members of society. But children are not merely unproductive adults-in-waiting. They are not the sum total of their loud, tantrum-having, messy, consuming, self-centred, needy selves. Children must be seen and heard, as people in their own right, because recognizing and acknowledging the humanity in all humans helps to undermine the systems of oppression and exploitation that bind us, and allows us to begin to imagine a new world.

Transforming movements for social change: from patriarchal constructions to collective approaches

In a world where the value of a human is defined by their production and consumption, respecting children as equals is unusual, not innate. And so we must work to transform our world to one with foundational values of care and collectivity and humanity. A critique that centres on the value of motherhood, of women, of parenting, and of children is and should be seen as an anti-capitalist critique, one that is aligned with and supportive of other struggles against racism, discrimination against the differently abled and the aged, and against colonialism, imperialism and their legacies and current practices in today's capitalist world. Our work to make the world a better place for "our" children must be a fight for everyone. Mothers' perspectives offer valuable critiques of the international order, of state and social institutions, and the ingrained behaviours and values that structure our lives.

While we point toward larger structural injustices, we can also critique the world framed by capital that we have to inhabit: our workplaces, our infrastructure, our social conventions and expectations. All facets of life demand scrutiny and change. The biggest challenge, perhaps, is scaling up: How do we get from these intensely private "family" spaces back to social movements? It's a real challenge, and one not solved merely by aggregation (adding and piecing them together until they are bigger and more encompassing). We have to put ideology back into the centre, to question how our ideological orientation in many ways replicates those of systems of oppression and exploitation.

As we work for transformation, we must also assess our methods and beliefs within our critiques and our protest movements. Seeing beyond the politics of waged labour is essential. Our movements too often mirror the dynamics and problems of the larger society. The focus of much of the political Left on waged work is actually a consequence of patriarchy; it is a sexist political outlook that has privileged what has historically been men's work while undermining and making invisible women's work. We need to understand the ways in which our non-waged caring and reproductive labour is essential to society and engage it as a site of struggle and resistance

This necessary extension of focus should be accompanied by an attention to the practical aspects of organizing. We need to recognize the value of every person in our movements. Currently, many movements often discount the work that members do if it isn't deemed "productive work." We rarely make space for children in our movements, nor do we accommodate parents' schedules (especially those of single parents). It's no secret that many conventional circles of self-identified activists are predominantly made up of college-aged youth who likely don't understand the pressures that parents face. These circles often make little attempt to understand that reality—instead choosing to insinuate that parents have been co-opted by the mainstream and de-radicalized. In reality, parents often see themselves as having even more at stake: a future for their children. Parents are torn between the need to care for their children in the here-and-now and the need to ensure a fair future for their children. They usually cannot take dramatic risks, such as facing jail time for engaging in direct action, for fear of having their children taken from them. This is doubly true for parents facing various forms of systemic and structural marginalization or oppression, whose capacities to parent are already called into question.

But a heightened awareness of the politics of motherhood and reproductive labour can also be a great energizer for social justice movements, broadening our sense of who "we" are and who we fight for, making us reach out beyond our own comfortable sense of existing community. Things like birth, death, and major life events can be incredibly politicizing experiences. And what's great about it is that we all experience them, albeit in very different ways, and thus it challenges our movements to include people across the life course and from different places and spaces, rather than the typical social cultures (e.g. union, student, punk rock) upon which the Left frequently draws. In a sense, it is a new set of spaces within which to organize, to struggle, to resist.

These questions we raise are part of a larger movement for change. Just as women's reproductive labour is central to capitalism, so too is it central to the transformation of society. Re-imagining motherhood gives us a chance to rethink and re-envision all aspects of our lives—from the struggle against austerity and the dismantling of the welfare state and social safety net, to the assaults on our communities and the social fabric that binds them. By looking at the politics of mothering we ground our struggle in our day-to-day life. We must always remember how fragile we are and how much we *all* need help. Ultimately, these politics are radical in the sense that they get to the root of it all, to the meaning of our existence as humans: what is of value in life, and how can we live in more interconnected ways?

CHAPTER FIVE

Prison in the spaces between us: Abolition, austerity, and the possibility of compassionate containments

Ardath J. Whynacht

ARDATH J. WHYNACHT is an artist, activist and professor living on unceded Mi'kmaw territory. She teaches at Mount Allison University and runs creative peer support programs both inside and outside of the federal prison system. She is currently working on "Insurgent Love," a SSHRC-funded research project that explores emotional labour and queer kinship as transformative practice.

But Rebellion
is the circle of a lover's hands
that must keep moving,
always weaving.

— Martín Espada[1]

Many of us have seen the footage of Ashley Smith being forcibly restrained by a half-dozen guards in combat suits with plexiglass face shields. Originally incarcerated as a teenager in New Brunswick for throwing crab apples at a postal worker, Ashley spent a total of four years in solitary confinement and was transferred 17 times between eight institutions in four different provinces while in federal custody. Ashley repeatedly attempted to harm herself, prompting "use of force" incidences. Management eventually gave the order that no one was to enter her cell while she was still breathing. Ashley died by self-strangulation in the Grand Valley Institution on October 19, 2007 while prison staff watched on surveillance cameras from outside the cell. Her death prompted public outcry over her treatment in the Canadian federal prison system. In December 2013, a coroner's inquest ruled her death to be a homicide. Video footage showing Ashley screaming while guards held her down in a solitary confinement cell painted a grim picture of what life was like for the nineteen-year-old in the Canadian prison system. Ashley's tragic death became a rare moment of widespread public concern about the treatment of prisoners. It was clear: what happened to Ashley was violence. State violence took the shape of restraints, forced sedation, long periods in solitary confinement and repeated "use of force" incidents inflicted by correctional officers. The surveillance footage served as evidence in the coroner's inquest into her death, but it also alerted the public that violence was alive and well in the prison system.

I have been teaching poetry in prisons for the past ten years. I began working in the maximum-security unit of a women's institution just a few short months after Ashley's death. Since then, I have worked with many women who struggle with self-harm inside the prison and inpatient mental health facilities. Ashley Smith had learning disabilities and was also diagnosed with Borderline Personality Disorder (BPD), a diagnosis that is drastically overrepresented in the prison population. At any given time most of the women in the unit where I teach meet the diagnostic criteria for BPD. Research shows that BPD patients are those who are most stigmatized in health care settings,[2] denied care,[3] and (although they represent approximately two percent of the general population) drastically overrepresented in the prison system. In a comprehensive review of the literature, Sansone and Sansone suggest, "collectively, these studies—all using specific measures for personality disorder assessment—suggest that approximately 25 to 50 percent of prisoners suffer from BPD".[4]

In 2010 I began an arts-based research project with women who have the diagnosis of BPD and who have spent time in secure care, either in the prison system or the mental health care system. This work has forced me to question my own position as a feminist prison abolitionist. Their experiences reveal problematic assumptions in abolitionist organizing and force us to examine a less visible, but no less tangible landscape of neglect outside the walls of the prison and hospital. Most women with the diagnosis of BPD have had repeated experiences of seeking care in the mental health care system and have been turned away. The violence they have experienced is more difficult to discern—it is the violence of neglect and abandonment. This violence is rendered unintelligible in critical spaces that frame violence as an assault on bodily autonomy or freedom. When you have been denied care, "autonomy" becomes a painful lived experience. In the context of neoliberal austerity since the 1980s, compassionate spaces of containment and support have dwindled, leaving those who desire institutional care alienated and subject to problematic notions of "self-care" and "positive thinking." In the following pages, I will reflect on how this work with women who have been diagnosed with BPD has disrupted and re-framed my position as a prison abolitionist and transformed my vision of a post-carceral future.

Autonomy as neoliberal violence

Academic critiques of the carceral state emerged in the mid-20th century. Michel Foucault's work on prisons and the birth of psychiatry gave rise to decades of critical scholarship that took aim at the organization of power in disciplinary societies. At the same time, Canadian sociologist Erving Goffman's work on total institutions brought widespread attention to the terrible conditions of the asylum—institutions that were bloated with ever increasing numbers of poor, disenfranchised, disabled and ill citizens who were forced to live in humiliating conditions of squalor.[5] Goffman's work became part of the deinstitutionalization movement, which sought to dismantle and close the asylum system in favour of community-based care. These foundational critiques of the prison and the psychiatric systems emerged during a historical peak in the number of incarcerated people in prisons and asylums. Bernard Harcourt points out that "the highest rate of aggregated institutionalization during the entire 20th century occurred in 1955 when almost 640 persons per 100,000 adults over age fifteen were institutionalized in asylums, mental hospitals, and state and federal prisons."[6] The deinstitutionalization movement was largely successful in forcing districts to close asylums, however, as many mental health advocacy groups and the Canadian Prison Ombudsman have pointed out, the closure of asylums led to a corresponding boom in the numbers of people labelled as mentally ill living in prisons. The story goes like this: as asylums closed, a period of mass incarceration emerged in the 1980s and 1990s, leading to a drastic overrepresentation of those labelled mentally ill people living in the prison system.

In the prison where I teach, it's hard to argue with that story. Med-line happens at 7pm for women living in general population and it stretches down a long hallway and out the door. In the max unit, my poetry students write quietly at the table, their hands moving across the page, forearms covered from wrist to elbow in purple stripes, traces left behind from decades of self-harm.

However, Liat Ben-Moshe, a prison abolitionist and disability studies scholar, argues that the story is not so simple. Ben-Moshe urges us to see the deinstitutionalization movement as an important case study in decarceration. Rather than seeing the widespread closure of asylums as a failure, she suggests "deinstitutionalization could be characterized not only as a process or an exodus of oppressed people outside the walls of institutions and into community living, but as a radical anti-segregationist philosophy."[7]

Ben-Moshe has done critical work in weaving together histories of deinstitutionalization with movements for prison abolition, but critique of the carceral state that positions deinstitutionalization as a successful social movement stands in stark contrast to the stories I had been hearing from women with the diagnosis of BPD. In 2010 I heard Ben-Moshe speak on a panel at the International Conference on Penal Abolition (ICOPA) in Ottawa. This was the point at which I began to question my own place within prison abolitionist organizing. I remember becoming hot, my face flushed. I started sweating as a room full of prison abolitionists began to consider the closure of asylums as a case study for decarceration. Until this moment, I considered the prison abolitionist movement to be my home. But as the discussion carried on, I struggled with a growing sense of incoherence between what I had been hearing from the women I was working with and the critiques that were being employed within the movement.

It was not that I disagreed with Ben-Moshe, it was simply a turning point for me, toward the realization that the language of autonomy in prison abolitionist movements reproduces neoliberal forms of violence against those whose lived experience has been one of neglect. The vision of justice deployed in this space was shaped by disableist privilege: if you've never *known* state "care," how can you begin to critique it? What are the consequences of calling deinstitutionalization a successful movement when those with complex and under-served diagnoses are fighting *for* these problematic forms of state intervention? I felt as if I was complicit in the violence of neoliberalism by being part of a movement that positioned deinstitutionalization as a success. Lived experience of BPD points to the harmful effects of consistent *invalidation* and *dismissal*. Continual denial of emotional suffering builds up painful relational structures that create emotional dysregulation and hypersensitivity. Lived experience of emotional dysregulation is that of pain and distress that is out of scale with normative expectations of how we are "supposed" to feel in a given situation. Feelings of insecurity, loss, depression and anger emerge unpredictably and in ways that create suicidal ideation and severe suffering. Women with BPD are a large part of the prison population—but dismissing their experiences with *needing* institutional care not only alienated them from abolition movements, it perpetuated the same harms they had experienced their entire lives—the denial of their emotional distress. I wanted to be part of an abolition movement that placed the concerns and lived experiences of incarcerated people *first*. By positioning deinstitutionalization as a "success," we are effectively dismissing and ignoring how harmful an absence of care has been in the lives of the women I was working with. Dismissal of emotional distress serves to mask trauma that is enacted through the carceral state. At this point I realized that I could not engage in these same mechanisms of emotional invalidation in my activist work.

Begging to get in

"Four times. Four times I went to the ER before I overdosed. They sent me home every time. I went into a coma. After that I was in the hospital a few weeks." I nod. This is a story I hear repeatedly. Borderline personality disorder is part of a class of "disorders" that go largely untreated in the mental health care system. Specific forms of talk therapy can be really helpful for BPD but our systems are only resourced to "prescribe and discharge." Early intervention programs for psychosis and support programs for bipolar disorder are commonplace, but women with BPD often spend years on waitlists for treatment, despite the fact that BPD is more common. BPD treatment requires talk therapy, which strains hospital budgets.

Once a week, we meet and make art together: we paint, write poems, and drink tea. Their stories are a living history of neglect, abandonment, dismissal, and invalidation. You can be bleeding from both wrists and sent home from the ER because your pain is not seen as "urgent" in triage. The development of BPD is partly attributed to life experiences with trauma and being raised in emotionally abusive or invalidating homes. Much of the violence experienced by women with BPD is the collateral (and intentional) damage done by patriarchy, white supremacy, and settler colonial cultures that value abstract intellectualism and dismiss emotional experience as a legitimate form of knowledge. The result is a painful choreography of emotional dysregulation, where their relationships with others trigger intense feelings of abandonment, despair, and anger. They are constantly being told that they are "over-reacting," their suffering is dismissed in both community and institutional spaces as "attention seeking" or melodramatic. I hear many stories from parents and partners of women with BPD who have fought, over and over again, to have their loved one admitted into secure care because they can't keep them safe from persistent attempts at suicide and self-harm. It is here that we can see Ashley Smith's experiences with self-harm as part of a bigger pattern of dysregulation and suffering. When I think about abolishing prisons and asylums, I remember the words of a parent, whose daughter had been denied inpatient care: "she tried to hang herself when she got home. They wouldn't admit her in the adult or children's system. I just didn't know what to do anymore." The violence of forced sedation is crystal clear. The violence of neglect and abandonment is much harder to discern unless you find yourself at the doors of a carceral institution, begging to get in. We can dismantle the buildings, brick by brick, but the carceral state will still exist in the spaces between us. We keep the carceral state alive by gaslighting its victims and denying the traumatic effects of living in a neoliberal culture that dismisses the misery created by capitalism.

Decades of austerity have slowly dismantled the remnants of a state-funded social safety net. At the same time, the practices of discipline, punishment and surveillance have become embedded in the fabric of every social institution—our families, our schools, our workplaces—there is no space that isn't part of what Michel Foucault has called "the carceral continuum."[8] Years of working with women with a complex and under-served diagnosis has drawn my attention to the ways in which neglect and abandonment function as carceral violence. However, many of the abolitionist critiques I have learned to deploy in my work as an activist rest on disableist notions of violence that are rooted in problematic notions of individual autonomy. These critiques emerged at a time in history when forced institutionalization was at an all-time high, yet, in perpetuating these critiques of the carceral state as it emerges in violation to our sense of bodily autonomy and freedom we are perpetuating the neoliberal violence of neglect and abandonment for those who have been most harmed by the dismantling of the welfare state. What are we to do with our sisters who want to harm themselves? Prisons and asylums are not compassionate spaces, but when we struggle with feeling that we can't keep ourselves safe from ourselves, where else are we to go? The urgency of suicidality begs us to respond. Anti-psychiatry narratives are alive and well in both activist and scholarly spaces, yet, if we follow Ben-Moshe's call to weave together anti-psychiatry social movements with prison abolitionist social movements, we risk alienating (and even harming) those with very real needs for some form of life-saving care. We perpetuate the harm of the carceral state by building movements that pretend that the emotional distress of suicidality and self-harm doesn't exist. By not putting this suffering at the centre of our movements, we replicate the mechanisms of emotional invalidation that are characteristic of neoliberal institutions.

Merri Lisa Johnson, a gender studies scholar who is "out" about her diagnosis with BPD, reminds us "there are reasons for emotional dysregulation. There are reasons for drinking and cutting, for smoking meth and lighting fires. There is a story that makes sense of all this."[9] She has cautioned activist communities against using simplistic arguments against psychiatry and institutional care. She points out that certain forms of care are a matter of life and death. Indeed, access to this care is usually reserved for young women with wealthy parents who have private medical insurance and can access psychiatric services outside the public healthcare system. As an abolitionist, I want to radically envision what "care" could look like outside the carceral model, but I want to do it in a way that keeps my friends alive so they can join the movement too. Critiques of biomedicalization in mental health have not led to meaningful changes in how emotional and psychological suffering is accepted and soothed in our communities. Indeed, judgement and critique of "big pharma" has often further marginalized those in our societies who have chosen to take psychiatric medication because it is helpful to them. We are quick to criticize over prescription of psychiatric medication, yet we take no issue with the provision of drugs for diabetes or heart conditions. Stigma within radical communities often manifests as skepticism about the validity of a particular diagnosis, which leaves the afflicted person feeling as if they should just "get over it" on their own because their diagnosis is just a false label from the psy-carceral system. This is deeply invalidating and echoes the gaslighting of neoliberal ideologies that render many forms of suffering invalid, such as the trauma related to sexual assault, over-work, or experiences of racism or patriarchy. We replicate neoliberal tropes of "positive thinking" as a solution to the effects of social trauma by telling suicidal friends to "think positive" or "just be happy." We know that trauma, mental illness and addiction must be understood as stemming from a complex interrelation of factors that are social, biological, emotional, and implicate human and non-human actors. Employing narrow social constructionist critiques against the medical system keeps our feet firmly planted on territory that was colonized by Descartes and perpetuated by colonial divisions of nature and culture. Critiquing the psy-industrial complex by framing a mental health diagnosis as an artefact of our oppression does little to acknowledge or heal the distress that we face.

Whether the cause is social or biological (or both), the suffering is still real. Understanding the trauma experienced through neglect and abandonment tells a more complex story about the harms of contemporary capitalism. As Lincoln (2006) points out, the contemporary mental health care system has completely transformed since the 1950s and denial of access to inpatient treatment is now the norm for the most marginalized members of our communities: "previous policies led to disproportionate rates of involuntary hospitalization among marginalized and powerless groups; these same groups are disproportionately denied access to psychiatric inpatient treatment."[10]

It's not the 1950s anymore. We need a new framework with which to account for and disrupt the carceral state. It is far easier to critique a mob of correctional officers holding down a screaming nineteen-year-old girl than it is to account for the ways in which other women like her are being turned away from secure mental health care. It is difficult to critique neglect when we frame violence as a violation of freedom, rather than the absence of compassionate containment. But how do we envision "care" without resorting to the discipline and punish model of the 1950s asylum or the super-prison of the 1980s? How do we dismantle the carceral state without perpetuating further invalidation or dismissal of the suffering of women like Ashley?

The prison is everywhere in an age of neoliberal neglect

In my work in the prison, I am always astounded by the affectionate ways in which some women refer to their time inside. Women in secure care and prisons often speak about their time inside as a moment when they began to heal, get treatment, and "come up for air" after long periods of survival and desperation on the outside. In some ways, this acceptance of incarceration and forced treatment is a way of meeting the demands of "rehabilitation" that forces them to submit to the will of the state in order to get parole or security privileges to attend group programs. However, a recent research project[11] at the University of Waterloo with incarcerated women tells a different story. Data from this project points out that the violence of prison life is a continuation of the violence of daily life in our communities. Prison doesn't seem so bad if we also face high rates of coercion, violence, and suffering in the community. If we want to build movements that are led by and responsive to the harms experienced by incarcerated and traumatized people, then we must acknowledge that the *prison is everywhere*. Under today's austere form of neoliberal capitalism, our communities are wastelands. The violence of the carceral state is re-enacted to varying degrees in our intimate lives, our workplaces, and our educational institutions. When we make a monster out of the prison or psychiatric care, we risk enabling or turning a blind eye to the carceral violence outside the prison and the hospital. Women with borderline personality disorder know this continuum of violence all too well: they are the most overrepresented psychiatric diagnosis in the prison system and have the highest rates of sexual assault, family violence, and other traumatic experiences perpetuated through structures of neoliberal capitalism. But given their experiences of neglect in every single social institution, how can we argue for prison abolition through the lens of autonomy and freedom? How can we continue to engage in critiques against psychiatry when some of the most marginalized women and femmes in our own movements are banging on the doors of the hospital and being turned away? If BPD is partly a consequence of experiencing other forms of state violence early in life, how do we justify the abolition of the very services they are asking for? How do we justify this as a project that works against state violence when we are alienating the survivors with such disableist critiques?

Towards compassionate containment

Perhaps our most important contemporary critiques of the carceral state come from Black feminists. Angela Davis draws our attention to the relationship between the violence in the prison and the violence of statehood: "how then can one expect the state to solve the problem of violence against women, when it constantly recapitulates its own history of colonialism, racism, and war?"[12] The carceral state is a snake eating its tail. Critical attention to the ways in which prisons enact white supremacy and represent what Michelle Alexander has called "the new Jim Crow" era disrupt any notion of "criminal justice" as an impartial arbiter of the moral good.[13] Angela Davis reminds us that prisons are the new slavery. However, critiques of racism in the prison industrial complex rest on the politics of the "visual." We can "see" disproportionate incarceration of Black and Indigenous peoples, just as we can "see" the violence done to Ashley on the floor of her cell.

It is much more difficult to formulate an understanding of what Esther Armah has called "emotional justice,"[14] which attends to the emotional wounds experienced by Black women in patriarchal white supremacy. The wounds from trauma, neglect, and abandonment are invisible. Those who are most afflicted by these invisible wounds usually face the most intense and unrelenting forces of race, gender and class oppression. Colonized and brutalized communities face some of the highest rates of suicide and self-harm. Attention to "emotional justice" and the invisible roots of the carceral state is a matter of life and death.

When we forego disableist notions of violence that rest on neoliberal ideals of individualist autonomy, we are able to hold space for the creation of new languages to account for the affective violence of contemporary capitalism. When we acknowledge neglect as a form of carceral violence, we no longer remain caught up in arguments about whether or not psychiatry is evil and can position the abolitionist project in response to the suffering produced at every stage of the carceral continuum. When we trace the roots of our allegedly individual "selves" to the pain we bury beneath the surface we become better able to think through the future in ways that liberate us from past violence. We become better equipped to envision radical alternatives to psychiatry and can embed peer support and emotional acknowledgement in our organizing.

For this reason, the territory of the *felt* experience of our relationships with each other can radically transform our capacity to give and receive love that is not bound up in militarized, privatized notions of security. Too often, the territory of *felt* experience is rendered invisible in everyday life. We end up building our movements around the most visible forms of violence and don't attend to the other planes of experience that drive us to keep building prisons and keep harming each other. Violence comes from distress, fear and (in)security, it is from *these places* that we seek out and desire walls and borders. We need to better account for the emotional roots of carceral violence. We need to develop a language to account for suffering that is not dependent on diagnostic manuals and stop drawing lines in the sand between communities and their institutions as if the monster of "the state" can be limited to the prison or the psych ward. When we are paralyzed with moral and emotional confusion over a sexual assault in our own community and don't know how to build a community response that furthers healing, we have reached the edges of ourselves. We must be impelled to restructure our patterns of relating to each other and redefine security in ways that account for existing trauma. When our loved ones are suicidal, we don't stand back and respect their "bodily autonomy," we hold them down, hard. We wrestle away the razor blade. We soothe them with our bodies. I want to be part of an abolitionist project that acknowledges a need for this kind of compassionate containment. Radical notions of compassionate containment would provide a necessary counterpoint to the carceral violence that Ashley experienced inside the prison.

It is only through deep and sustained friendships with women with borderline personality disorder that I have come to this position as an abolitionist. I am now invested in working within the terrain of emotional experience as a deliberate strategy to disrupt the carceral state. In our work together, we have tried to imagine what trauma-informed spaces would look like in a time of austerity. Life in contemporary capitalism leaves us feeling as if we are floating in space, set adrift from the safety net of kinship networks and social support. When I think about the abolitionist project I want to see in the future, it looks like constellations in the desolation of space. When we imagine a post-carceral future together, we don't just envision a world free from shackles and restraints where we're all equally free to cross state borders. We imagine broad and vast networks of *containment* and care that are responsive to and in dynamic relationship with our most intimate needs for kinship and emotional security. We imagine a different kind of radical safety net. Attention to emotional justice reminds us that the prison emerges in the spaces between us. It is not enough to focus on dismantling the architectures of confinement, we must also be attentive to new forms of violence in contemporary capitalism that leave us all in a wasteland of exhaustion, insecurity, and acute trauma from state, economic, and interpersonal violence.

Notes

1. Martin Espada, "Rebellion is the Circle of a Lover's Hands (Pellín and Nina)," *Rebellion is the Circle of a Lover's Hands* (Curbstone Press, 1990), 26.

2. Joel Paris, "Why Psychiatrists are Reluctant to Diagnose Borderline Personality disorder," *Psychiatry, 4*(1) (2007): 35-39.

3. Dana Becker, *Through the Looking Glass: Women and Borderline Personality Disorder.* (Boulder: Westview Press, 1997); Merri Lisa Johnson, *Girl in Need of a Tourniquet: A Memoir of Borderline Personality Disorder*, (Berkley: Seal Press, 2010).

4. Randy A. Sansone and Lori A. Sansone, "Borderline Personality and Criminality," *Psychiatry*, 6(10) (2009): 16-20.

5. Erving Goffman, *Asylums: Essays on the Situation of Mental Patients and Other Inmates* (Norwell: Anchor Press, 1961).

6. Bernard E. Harcourt, "From the Asylum to the Prison: Rethinking the Incarceration Revolution," *Texas Law Review* 84 (2005): 1754.

7. Liat Ben-Moshe, "Deinstitutionalization: A Case Study in Carceral Abolition," *Scapegoat Journal* 7 (2014): 22.

8. Michel Foucault, *Discipline and Punish: The Birth of the Prison* (New York: Vintage Books, 1995).

9. Johnson, *Girl in Need of a Tourniquet*, 155.

10. Alisa Lincoln, "Psychiatric Emergency Room Decision-making, Social Control and the 'Undeserving Sick'," *Sociology of Health & Illness, 28*(1) (2006): 622-623.

11. "Uncertain Futures." https://uwaterloo.ca/uncertain-futures/.

12. Angela Y. Davis, *Are Prisons Obsolete?* (New York: Seven Stories Press, 2003).

13. Michelle Alexander, *The New Jim Crow: Mass Incarceration in the Age of Colorblindness* (New York: The New Press, 2012).

14. Dalila-Johari Paul, "Emotional Justice: What Black Women Want and Need" *The Guardian*, December 3, 2015, https://www.theguardian.com/world/2015/dec/03/emotional-justice-what-black-women-want-and-need.

CHAPTER SIX

Passages from the interregnum: Countering austerity and authoritarianism in theory, education, and print

An interview with Jerome Roos

JEROME ROOS is a writer, publisher, and activist. In 2010, he founded *ROAR Magazine*, an independent journal of social movements and radical democratic politics, which he continues to edit together with his friend Joris Leverink. Jerome is currently a post-doctoral researcher in political economy at the Department of Sociology of the University of Cambridge, where he is finishing a book on the structural power of finance in sovereign debt crises (under contract with Princeton University Press). Read more about his work at JeromeRoos.com. Max Haiven interviewed Jerome in April, 2017.

MAX HAIVEN: I want to start by asking you to reflect on the most recent debacle of this particular moment: the recent French election, which nicely encapsulates the false struggle between the neoliberal financialization of Macron and the horrific, racist authoritarianism of Le Pen. What happened there, and how did we get to a moment when these false options were in front of us? Maybe you could also comment on the limits of the mainstream response to Macron's victory as some form of salvation.

JEROME ROOS: Let me begin by saying that I have become increasingly troubled this past year by the dominant framing of recent political events. The response we've seen from the centrist establishment and the mainstream media to Brexit and Trump is fairly indicative of this. Basically, the entire political narrative over the past year has been constructed around this notion that an unstoppable "populist wave" is washing across the world, as if the rising tide of populist politics is the real problem here, as opposed to the wider storm that gave rise to it. `

Clearly, there are a number of problems with this framing of ongoing political developments. First of all, it ends up focusing all the attention on the electoral successes and administrative inanities of "the populists," as opposed to the much more significant failings of the centrist establishment, which made the populists' recent electoral victories possible to begin with. Secondly, it ends up conflating a number of different phenomena—like the rise of Bernie Sanders and Jeremy Corbyn on the Left, with the electoral successes of Donald Trump and Nigel Farage on the right— that are actually wildly divergent in their politics and obviously incomparable in every respect apart from their scathing anti-establishment rhetoric. Thirdly, and this is what most concerns me with respect to the French elections, by framing the present crisis in terms of a "populist wave" we risk letting the underlying culprit—neoliberalism—off the hook.

We are seeing this now with Macron's victory: by framing the problem narrowly in terms of a "populist wave," it becomes very easy for the neoliberal establishment to then claim that the defeat of the populist candidate hails the reversal of the populist tide. We already saw this reaction following the 2017 elections in the Netherlands, when the Islamophobic far-right extremist Geert Wilders came second even though he had been polling first for a while in the lead-up to the vote. And so when the centre-right neoliberals "defeated" Wilders, EU leaders and the international media collectively let out a sigh of relief: "Ah, the Netherlands has brought the populist wave to a halt! The Brexit/Trump effect won't spread to continental Europe!" The same is now being said about Le Pen's defeat. By framing the problem in terms of populism, the victory of the neoliberal candidate can then be construed as the end of the crisis.

Clearly this is wishful thinking at its most dangerous. If anything, the fact that Le Pen made it to the second round of the French presidential elections actually confirms that the nationalist far-right is rapidly gaining force in one of Europe's biggest and most advanced capitalist democracies. The fact that some 11 million people went out to vote for her—twice as many as voted for her father in the run-off of the 2002 presidential elections—should make it blatantly clear that right-wing xenophobes have enormous political momentum behind them right now. Moreover, we are seeing this development across the world, with the rise of the authoritarian and nationalist right in Russia, Turkey, India, Brazil—not to mention the US and UK. So this is a global phenomenon with complex structural dimensions. It doesn't simply go away with the supposed "defeat" of a single populist candidate in a single electoral cycle in a single country. In fact, as for France, the main concern here is that Macron's neoliberal policies will pave the way for Le Pen to put up a successful opposition and defeat him in the next elections of 2022.

So that brings me to the first part of your question about the underlying causes of all of this and what's really happening here. How did we get to a moment where these false choices between centre-right neoliberalism and far-right nationalism are now before us? The way I see it, the crisis we are currently living through is structural in nature. What we should really be looking at, then, is not the outcome of a single election but, rather, the more long-term trends that have brought us to this point—not just in the last couple of years since the global financial crisis, but ever since the previous structural crisis of the 1970s, when the advanced capitalist economies suffered from falling profit margins, stagnant growth, rising inflation and social unrest. Back then, segments of the political and economic elite responded to the crisis by pursuing a temporary neoliberal "fix" that included the liberalization of capital flows and the deregulation of the financial sector. The outcome was what we now call globalization and financialization.

For a while, this neoliberal fix allowed the establishment to stave off the intensifying social conflicts of the late 1960s and early 1970s. For one, globalization allowed for the offshoring of production to the East, thereby breaking the back of the powerful Western labour movement and Western social democracy, which kept demanding higher wages and hence depressing capitalists' profit margins. At the same time, offshoring to countries with much lower wages and labour standards also allowed capitalists to flood the world market with cheap "Made in China" consumer goods: think of your iPhone or the t-shirt you're wearing. Meanwhile, this related process of financialization dramatically increased the availability of cheap credit within the system, which allowed capitalist firms and states to insert new resources into the distributional conflicts that had shaken the system in the 1970s, allowing workers and middle-class households to maintain a consumerist lifestyle even in the face of stagnant wages and, in many cases, rising debts and falling living standards. The neoliberal counterrevolution that took off in full force in the 1980s was all about "keeping up appearances" on a global scale.

Of course there were many more dimensions to this transition that I cannot go into here, but the crucial point, I believe, is that these temporary "fixes" came at a price, placing a number of time bombs underneath the system: rising inequality, growing precarity, exploding debts, a dramatic expansion of corporate power, the loss of national sovereignty and democratic control over money and finance, and so on. Meanwhile, growing numbers of people who had little hope of earning decent wages in the countries where they were born began to migrate towards the countries of the core in the hope of finding more stable employment there. It is important to point out that these numbers were relatively small by historical standards (the late-19th century, for instance, saw a much larger influx of migrants into the United States). Moreover, research has shown that the effects of migration on employment and economic performance are, if anything, positive—meaning "they" didn't come over to steal "our" jobs. Nevertheless, the arrival of migrants provided convenient fodder for the racist cannons of the far-right. It is not a coincidence, then, that globalization went hand-in-hand with the rise of new nationalisms.

Nevertheless, for a brief period at least, the temporary neoliberal fix appeared to work pretty well. In the 1990s it even led to a widespread belief in the ultimate triumph of capitalist democracy and the immortal supremacy of a globalized liberal world order under US hegemony. But then, quite suddenly, within the space of less than a decade, two historic ruptures shook that naïve belief to its very core: September 11 and the global financial crisis. They first pulled the rug from underneath the utopian "conflict-free" myth of the "end of history" that had been concocted by the neoliberal establishment and its acolytes in the wake of the fall of the Soviet Union. It led to a dramatic expansion of state powers in surveillance, empire-building, and policing, and helped catalyze the rise of what some have called "authoritarian neoliberalism." The subsequent horrors of Abu Ghraib and Guantánamo Bay revealed the shambolic nature of Western democracy.

The second rupture—the collapse of Lehman Brothers and the economic and political fallout that followed in its wake—finally exposed financialization for the inherently unstable dynamic it really is. By responding to the crisis with bank bailouts and austerity, the establishment then generated the preconditions for an explosion of distributional conflict and a profound legitimation crisis of representative institutions. Suddenly, capitalism's existential problems of the 1970s came back to haunt the system with a vengeance. The only thing still keeping the show on the road is an absolutely unprecedented expansion of liquidity into the global financial system through the "unconventional monetary policies" of the world's leading central banks—which have in turn blown up a new series of asset price bubbles that appear to be unrivalled in their size and the possible damage they could wreak upon the world economy at the next sign of crisis.

So it is slowly beginning to dawn on the political and corporate establishment that there is no going back to the neoliberal glory days of the 1990s. Western billionaires are buying up bolt holes in New Zealand for a reason: they are growing increasingly anxious about the popular backlash to three decades of failed short-term fixes to capitalism's profound contradictions. Globalization and financialization have run out of steam, and even if its neoliberal defendants succeed in patching it up and keeping the show on the road just a little bit longer, the only thing that will come out of it is an explosion of social discontent and political polarization, which will in turn require further expansions of state control to help "keep the peace." Democracy will be further eroded, insofar as that is still imaginable, and basic liberal freedoms may go with it.

So I think it's fair to say that we currently find ourselves in a sort of Gramscian interregnum, in which the old world is dying and the new cannot be born. And as Gramsci wrote from within his fascist prison cell during the last great interregnum, in between the two World Wars, such phases of transition tend to be "the time of monsters," in which "a great variety of morbid symptoms appear." This is the context in which we have to understand the rise of the new crop of racist authoritarians like Donald Trump and Marine Le Pen. And this is the context in which we have to assess the likelihood of someone like Hillary Clinton or Emmanuel Macron offering a credible remedy. Once you put one and two together, you quickly see that their proposed solutions simply don't add up. The neoliberals propose to defeat the far-right with more of the same—even though their neoliberal "fixes" have long since run out of steam, and any further application of its fundamentally flawed principles is only likely to end in disaster.

MH: You spent a lot of time in Greece, thinking about Greece, and following the ups and downs of the Greek resistance to austerity. What do you think the example of Greece has to teach us in this moment, both in terms of the collapse of neoliberalism and the rise of austerity (and worse), and also about how movements should be approaching this moment?

JR: In many respects, Greece has been on the frontlines of some of the most important political and economic dynamics of our times. One of them, obviously, is the turn toward an increasingly aggressive form of neoliberalism; one that the Global South had already been exposed to for 30 or 40 years, ever since the start of the international debt crisis in the 1980s and the rise of the Washington Consensus in the 1990s. The brutal logic of outright dispossession has now finally crept up toward the heartland of European capitalism.

This increasingly aggressive form of neoliberalism has been around for a while, but it began to be properly institutionalized in Greece in 2010 with the first bailout agreement, which compelled the Greek government to push through a number of structural reforms and fiscal adjustments in order to free up the maximum amount of domestic resources for foreign debt servicing. Since most of the Greek debt was held by European banks at this point, especially French and German banks, the management of the Greek crisis also tells us a lot about the consequences of the financial "fix" that I discussed earlier. One of the consequences of financialization has been to make it increasingly costly for countries to simply default on their external debts, and increasingly unattractive for their creditors to grant them orderly debt relief.

There's a very stark contrast, in this respect, between how different international debt crises have historically been resolved. If you look at the 1930s, for instance, or much of the 19th century, it was actually very common for a heavily indebted country—when it went into crisis after a major economic shock—to simply suspend payments on its foreign debts. That was not only a move made by progressive governments; it was a policy pursued across the board by governments of various political stripes. In fact, the imposition of a unilateral debt moratorium was considered normal, part of the rules of the game. The same is still true of businesses today: if a bank lends too much money to a private firm, and that firm subsequently faces solvency issues, the debts of that firm will be restructured and the bank will have to take losses. It happens all the time. But at the level of sovereign lending—lending to national governments—that policy option has now been precluded: there's an insistence that all governments must and will repay their debts in full.

So in that respect, the Greek debt crisis, and the way in which European policymakers have responded to it, speaks to a major transformation in the global political economy that makes it increasingly difficult for nation-states to pursue an autonomous economic policy, because the power of finance has become so incredibly overwhelming that national autonomy has been hollowed out, and as a result the sovereign authority of governments is steadily undermined. The problem, of course, is that the only democratic institutions we currently have—however imperfect they already were prior to globalization and financialization—are fundamentally dependent on this notion of national sovereignty. If a democratically elected government cannot pursue an autonomous fiscal or monetary policy, elections cease to have any real substantive meaning. The German Finance Minister, Wolfgang Schäuble, was simply being forthright when he stated that Greece's elections should not be allowed to change the country's economic policies. This is the point: globalization and financialization completely hollow out the little bit of democratic responsiveness that ever existed in the advanced capitalist societies, and Greece has become a paradigmatic case of that development in recent years.

Of course another important part of the story is the way in which the Greek debt was subsequently repaid in the years since 2010. The policies that have been pushed onto Greece by the European creditor powers and the International Monetary Fund have largely spared some of the wealthiest and most powerful segments of Greek society, at the expense of working- and middle-class Greeks whose living standards have been eviscerated as a result of the austerity measures, tax hikes, and privatizations that were demanded by the so-called *Troika* of foreign lenders. Here, again, we see an extreme manifestation of the tendency towards widening inequality and oligarchic power under neoliberalism—a development that, in varying forms and degrees, can be witnessed across the globe, in the North and South alike.

By deflecting the costs of the crisis onto ordinary Greeks, the austerity measures demanded by the *Troika* also produced a very deep legitimation crisis of the Greek political system. The response on the part of society was a spectacular cycle of struggles between

2010 and 2012, which saw the social movements and the Greek Left organize a wave of general strikes and an incredible succession of mass demonstrations that sometimes ended in violent riots, but that also contained some very creative aspects: the construction of new economic and social forms of self-organization, the development of alternative solidarity economies, various forms of mutual aid and solidarity work with refugees, and countless other ways to cope with the consequences of the crisis and build a new world within the crumbling interstices of the old. Where the state and the market retreated, the movements reinvigorated the commons.

On this point, as well, the Greek experience has been exemplary of broader international trends. The occupation of Syntagma Square in May and June 2011, for instance, prefigured the global Occupy movement; while the election of the Syriza government in 2015—despite its subsequent defeat—somehow acted as a premonition of the rise of Bernie Sanders in the US and Jeremy Corbyn in the UK. So what we've been seeing in Greece, on the one hand, is this extremely anti-democratic tendency to push all the costs of the crisis onto ordinary Greeks and, on the other hand, the emergence of these new social movements, these new popular initiatives and this realignment of political forces that has shaken the old establishment parties to their very core. The dark underside of these developments has been the ascent of a neo-Nazi force, Golden Dawn, as one of the largest parties in the Greek parliament. Once again, Greece's political experience prefigured broader international trends in this respect.

A further point on which the Greek experience has been very instructive was the dramatic standoff between Syriza and its European creditors in the summer of 2015. In my view, the defeat of Greece's short-lived anti-austerity experiment in 2015 speaks to two key issues: first, the structural constraints on state action within the Eurozone, the European Union and the global political economy more generally; and second, the question of Left strategy within the context of these fundamentally asymmetric power relations. On both counts, Syriza's official position was ultimately self-defeating: ever since narrowly losing the 2012 elections, they basically said: "If you elect us, we're going to give you the best of both worlds: we're going to keep you inside the Eurozone, fully integrated into the circuits of global capital, but at the same time we're going to bring an end to these disastrous austerity measures and give you back your dignity." It was always obvious that one of these two promises would eventually have to give.

For about two or three years after the lost elections of 2012, the Left focused all its attention on the political project of winning state power, which eventually happened in January 2015. But over the same period the social movements partially demobilized and lost much of their original force and dynamism. By the time Syriza came to power, there was no longer the level of mass mobilization that had characterized the 2011-12 period and that had put the political system under enormous pressure *from below*. At the same time, in 2015 the European creditor powers still exerted enormous pressure on the Syriza government *from above*, hoping to thereby force it into submission. Basically, the Europeans were terrified that Greece might set a precedent that could be followed in Spain and elsewhere, perhaps even in Italy and France. If Syriza was allowed to succeed in renegotiating its debts and the conditions of its bailout, it might completely unravel the Eurozone austerity regime that had been so painfully constructed over the past five years. That, in turn, would have profoundly upset the immense power asymmetry between the creditor states and the debtor states, undermining Germany's dominant position within the bloc and empowering those pursuing a more progressive redistributive approach.

So here you have this epic confrontation between the Syriza government and the European creditor powers throughout the first half of 2015, which finally culminates in the referendum of July, where suddenly this incredible outpouring of popular energy re-emerges from the base. People headed back to Syntagma Square in the hundreds of thousands, urging the government never to surrender—and if need be, to defy its lenders and stop paying the debt. Given the overwhelming result of the referendum, it seems that at some point in July 2015 there was actually a small window for the government to radicalize its stance in the debt negotiations or even pursue a radical rupture with its creditors. The people indicated that they were ready for this—in fact, they were lightyears ahead of their supposedly "radical" Left government.

But the problem was that, by that point, Tsipras and his inner circle were already so far in, and the economic situation had deteriorated so much—with the European Central Bank having effectively shut down the Greek banking system following mass capital and deposit flight, leading to extreme financial turmoil—that the Syriza government essentially freaked out, especially the more centrist elements within the administration. The source of

Tsipras' paralysis, in my view, is that he was not at all prepared for the ferocity of the creditors' response. When we personally asked him, in late 2014, what he would do if Madame Merkel didn't give in to his demands for a renegotiation of the debt, he simply said, with a wry smile: "This is a game of chicken, and we are not going to be the first to blink." There was a woeful underestimation of the creditors' resolve to crush his radical-Left government and a dramatic over-estimation of Greece's leverage in the negotiations. An official at the finance ministry later admitted as much when he reflected on the capitulation with four simple words: "we underestimated their power."

The truth is, Tsipras never wanted to abandon the euro, and Greece was never going to get reprieve within the Eurozone, so his position was always already a contradictory one that could only ever end in either a full rupture or a full capitulation. But, perhaps if Tsipras and his inner circle had taken seriously the need to develop a back-up plan that would have allowed the government and the economy to continue functioning in the absence of foreign credit and European Central Bank liquidity, they might have had more self-confidence and been more willing to draw the result of the referendum to its logical conclusion. This was essentially the position of Finance Minister Yanis Varoufakis, who resigned when it became clear that Tsipras and his inner circle had no interest in escalating the confrontation with the creditors after the referendum results became known. The Left Platform, a minority grouping within Syriza, was hoping for an outright rupture. But ultimately the lack of preparation empowered those like Deputy Prime Minister Dragasakis, rumored to be close to the banks, whose preferred outcome was always simply to roll over and surrender. These were the people who finally got their way.

The Greek experience therefore holds some very important implications for Left strategy. Clearly, the social-democratic route—aiming for compromise with uncompromising capitalist powers—has long since been foreclosed by the changing balance of power and the virtual elimination of national policy autonomy. The challenge the Left now faces is to develop a new strategic approach that is capable of actually rebuilding its collective power from below and regaining a degree of autonomy from global financial markets and international organizations. As long as a country like Greece is dependent on outside funding to keep servicing its external debts, and as long as it depends on a "foreign" central bank for financial stability, over which it cannot exercise any democratic control, the power asymmetries virtually exclude the possibility of a democratically responsive policy decision. In order to advance, then, the Left must be willing to pursue a much more radical rupture with the status quo—and that, in turn, will require extensive preparation, not just in terms of policy, but also in terms of popular resilience. Left strategy therefore cannot be separated from the questions of social reproduction, of grassroots mobilization, of popular participation in the political process.

So Greece has been at the forefront of all of these developments and debates for years—which is why I am so terribly sad to see that the defeat of the first Syriza government has almost entirely killed the international Left's interest in the country. It seems self-evident to me that we need to keep engaging with the country not in spite of but precisely *because* of the defeat of Syriza's short-lived anti-austerity experiment. In many ways, not least in terms of the so-called refugee crisis, Greece remains the crucible of the tumultuous times we are living through. And so I think the European Left in particular has a strong obligation to keep exerting pressure on the EU to provide debt relief. But, perhaps even more importantly, we have to learn the right lessons from the Greek experience and adapt those to our own contexts.

MH: What was it that allowed for your radical imagination to emerge? How did you become interested in movements, and the study of struggle?

JR: The seedling was probably there from a relatively young age, and I was always "political" in the sense of being interested in politics from a decidedly Left-wing perspective. But I think a foundational moment in my process of *intellectual* radicalization was the crisis of 2008—both the ways in which that challenged some long-standing presumptions about global capitalism, and the ways in which social movements responded to the crisis.

In terms of the origins of my radical imagination, I would point towards my own education at quite a unique school in the Netherlands; a place called *De Werkplaats Kindergemeenschap*, or the Workplace Children's Community, which was founded by the Dutch pacifist, anarchist, and educational reformer Kees Boeke. Boeke had been very active in the anti-war movement during the 1910s, and he had a particular analysis—widespread in anarchist, socialist and communist circles at the time—that the Great War was the result of the confluence of global capitalism and state power. Living in London at the time, he had become increasingly disillusioned by the failures of his pacifist activism to achieve its key objectives through established political channels. So in the early 1920s he and his wife—Beatrice Cadbury, one of the heirs of the Cadbury chocolate empire—took out a long-term lease on a piece of land in a town called Bilthoven, just outside of Utrecht, and they started what you could think of as a kind of commune for pacifist families from the Netherlands and elsewhere who wanted to live together and try to pursue a different way of life that was organized outside of state institutions.

The decision to start a pacifist community was partly just a romantic ideal, but it was also a direct response to the exercise of state power. Boeke had stopped paying taxes, since large amounts of tax money went to the military. The government responded by refusing him access to public transport, denying his children entry to public school, and basically excluding him from many public services that he would otherwise have had a right to as a citizen. His response was to self-organize education for his kids and those of a number of other pacifists who were in a similar position. As the years went by, Boeke developed a pedagogical approach which he called Sociocracy. Unlike liberal democracy, which is necessarily mediated through a *demos*, or a politically constructed notion of "the people" that is always susceptible to redefinition in nationalistic terms, Boeke envisioned a form of democracy that was at once more direct and more universal. Inspired by the Quaker values of his wife, he developed the idea that important decisions should be taken by the *socios*—the people who are part of the community—through a participatory and consensual process. So he established a form of direct democracy within this schooling system and within this community that would allow children to be made conscious, at a very early age, of the importance and responsibilities of active participation in social life.

By the time I entered *De Werkplaats* in the 1990s it had already become absorbed within the public education system and resembled something closer to an alternative Montessori school, but it still retained some of its early social values. It had funny aspects: we were supposed to address our teachers informally by their first names, and using the more casual pronouns. They weren't called "teachers"; they were called co-workers, and the students were called workers. The main decision-making body—of course it wasn't a real decision-making body, but a highly symbolic structure nonetheless—was what they called the *Werkersraad*, the workers' council, which was a body where the students would come together to discuss important matters about their school and their education. This was all conceived at a time when the council communism of the Dutch astronomer and revolutionary theorist Anton Pannekoek was quite big in the Netherlands. But even in my time, it was still a very community-oriented type of education, very egalitarian in nature and focused on cooperation, democratization and creative self-expression. Some of my old school friends still joke about "our anarchist youth." It was a unique experience in the Netherlands. The kids who went there were mostly the kids of intellectuals, artists—it was a relatively white school, but it was quite socially and politically conscious in those respects.

So I would say that the seeds of a radical imagination were probably already present at an early age. I was still in high school when the Iraq War started, for instance, and remember being strongly outraged by it. But at the same time, I think that growing up as a middle-class kid in any kind of Western society, the normal level of consciousness you're going to be socialized into is that of left-liberalism, at best, until you experience a genuine process of radicalization—something that viscerally exposes you to the profound injustices and fundamental irrationalities of capitalist society. For me, that more personal experience came in a couple of waves.

The first one was in university when I went on exchange to the University of Bologna in Italy. Bologna has historically been a centre of the communist Left in Italy, but also of the student movements, and of course the *Autonomia* movement in the 1960s and 70s. They call it "Bologna the Red" for that reason—it's a very Left-wing city. In addition to being the oldest in Europe, its university is also very radical in some of its positions—not the university itself but its student body (at least at the time). In 2005 there was an occupation of the university in response to a number of educational reforms pursued by the Berlusconi government, so the first thing I was exposed to upon arriving in Italy was an occupied Political Science faculty where the curriculum had been taken over by the student body. The first classes I attended were organized by students, sympathetic PhDs and professors—courses on Marx, on student activism, any kind of topic you can imagine. That struggle culminated in a massive march on Rome and a brutal police crackdown. I was 19 at the time; I had been following the earlier Seattle and Genoa marches from afar as a teenager, but this was the first time I was directly confronted with that type of state violence at a major protest. So this was a formative experience, I would say.

While I always felt this innate inclination towards the radical Left, it wasn't really until 2008 that I started to form a more coherent and theoretically informed vision of the world. I was studying political economy in London at the time when Lehman Brothers collapsed, so my Master's degree there basically became a crash course on the global financial crisis and I became fascinated by capitalism's tendency to produce this massive instability, and the way that governments respond to this instability by deflecting the costs of adjustment onto the population-at-large in order to save the powerful and wealthy segments of the population. That, plus my own exploding student debt and the fact that we lost our parental home sometime before the crisis, led me to take a strong interest in Marxian theories of finance, and eventually the work of David Harvey and Marx himself—as well as other key texts that were very important for me in forming a more coherent worldview and a more substantive critique of capitalism.

Eventually, those readings motivated me to start doing a PhD and set up a blog, which I called *Reflections on a Revolution*— which later became *ROAR Magazine*. For my PhD, I carried out a comparative-historical research project on the Greek debt crisis, trying to account for the relative decline in the incidence of unilateral default by developing a novel approach to the structural power of finance. With *ROAR*, I simply wanted to start sharing some of my own analyses of the global financial crisis and the mobilization of social movements in response to it. It was 2010 or 2011 and I was still kind of naïve in many respects; if I read my older texts there was definitely a degree of intellectual immaturity, and an unconscious hangover of previous liberal preconceptions. I would say that it wasn't until after the European anti-austerity mobilizations of 2011-12, in which I actively participated, especially in Athens and Madrid, that I really started thinking in more theoretical terms about capitalism, movement organizing, and Left strategy.

I guess that's the phase I'm still in now—radicalization is an unfolding process. I'm probably going to look back 10 years from now and identify more points where I changed my mind or evolved in my analyses. Participating in and paying close attention to concrete struggles has always been very important for me in that respect—in teaching me, pedagogically, what's possible and what's not possible, what the challenges are, what the opportunities are. I don't think it's possible—or at least it's not very wise—to become radical or theorize social change in a vacuum; it's always in a dialectical interplay with collective processes of struggle that the most creative ideas and the most interesting analyses begin to emerge.

MH: *ROAR* has since emerged as a key venue for critical reporting and debate on precisely these themes and is often cited as one of a new generation of radical publications that are framing the crucial discussions of strategy and solidarity not only in Europe, but globally. I wanted to ask you about your thinking regarding editing and sustaining an alternative publication in this day and age, this media ecology.

JR: It's quite funny because I'm sometimes asked this question—to talk about the publication itself and my thinking about the role of media activism—but I have never really reflected on it as much as I probably should have, and I often feel that I'm not really able to give an intelligent or satisfying answer to the question. I'm not a media expert, nor a social movement scholar, and I'm not someone who has thought an awful lot about publications and the function that they fulfill within the broader ecology of social and political activism. I see myself as a writer who is extremely interested in capitalism, its crises and its contestation. That "naturally" pushes me in a direction where I try to engage with the world through words. And being a kind of long-winded author who is quite critical of the way that world is organized at present, I logically ended up writing long and winding invectives against financial capitalism that no mainstream outlet would run. So if I wanted to get them published I didn't really have any choice: I had to set up my own.

Initially, when I started *ROAR* it was just my personal political blog—a space for reflection on the global financial crisis and its consequences. But over time, as powerful new movements began to emerge—starting with the Arab Spring, then the Southern European anti-austerity mobilizations, then the Occupy movement, then the mass demonstrations in Turkey and Brazil, and so on—this platform suddenly gained far more traction than I could ever have imagined when I started it. Friends began to ask me if I would run their pieces on the blog, and *ROAR* gradually became a space where others could share their ideas and analyses too. From there, it just grew organically: some of these contributors would write more pieces and became regular contributors. Some of the regular contributors became editors, and one of the editors Joris Leverink, my good friend and former housemate from Amsterdam who is currently living in Istanbul—now co-edits and manages the publication with me on a day-to-day basis.

Of course, there have been times where we stopped to look back and reflect on *ROAR*'s evolution, or tried to understand what's been happening within the movements and figure out how can we insert ourselves in future struggles, and so on. But much of the publication's growth has been organic, without me really reflecting on it from the perspective of a media theorist or someone with a particular interest in magazine publishing. It was actually never really my intention to become a full-time magazine editor; I just started out as a writer and eventually began to receive so many submissions and take on so many other responsibilities related to running a print magazine—from order fulfillment to customer service to communications with authors, designers, printers and distributors—that the editorial responsibilities kind of took over.

At some point, around mid-2013, we did have to make an important decision because the publication began to outgrow its roots as a blog. It was attracting a growing audience and an expanding base of contributors, and we felt that our old web design wasn't really up for the standards of the quality of our content anymore. So we decided to build a new website, which then brought with it a whole host of questions about what type of platform we should build. We felt that what was needed was a platform that, instead of simply providing news and spectacular images about the latest protest or strike, should focus on background, theoretical analysis, and strategy. So we decided to try to decouple ourselves from the social media news cycle and the immediate pressure to respond to current affairs, and said, "okay, let's identify a couple of important developments in the world today, and try to analyze some of the defining struggles around those themes and the possibilities for radical transformation within these domains."

That ultimately led to the idea to launch a limited number of special issues structured around specific questions—like the revival of the commune-form, the future of work, the rule of finance, the expansion of state control, the rise of the far-right, the politics of urban transformation, and so on. Since we were going to do these thematic issues anyway, we figured it would be even better if we also printed them and allowed people to subscribe—this is how the idea for the print magazine was born. So once the new website was finally launched in 2015 after two years of fundraising, design and development, we invited a bunch of scholar-activists, movement organizers, and independent journalists from around the world to contribute pieces on some of the most important challenges facing our movements today, and to enter into a debate with one another on how the broader Left can begin to turn the tide.

The magazine's initial successes have kind of exceeded our expectations. We have so far brought out five issues (six if you include the online-only Issue #0), and are currently working on our sixth one. We now have enough subscribers to pay for the whole operation (in terms of printing, distribution, overhead and contribution for authors, designers and illustrators), although Joris and I are still working on the project as volunteers. That said, despite the self-funding nature of the publication as such, we have kind of arrived at a point where other work-related responsibilities are making it more and more difficult for us to keep up the intensive work required to sustain the quarterly issues. So we're going to be winding down the print publication at the end of 2017 to be able to spend more time on research, writing, and other related projects.

Meanwhile, we're going to have to think hard about what the post-print version of *ROAR* is going to evolve into, and how we can insert ourselves into the upcoming struggles now that we have the rise of the far-right, the Trump presidency, and all the challenges that come with that.

MH: So now we find ourselves trying to figure out what to do at this dangerous juncture. In spite of the fact that you guys in *ROAR* and so many of us, in various ways, have been warning that this relentless boot of austerity would lead to uprisings—not just of the Left but of the right—we've still been caught on the back foot by the recent dark turn. There's a real questioning everywhere of how we should organize and how we should respond. It's a fascinating time to be alive, and a terrifying time to be alive as well. I wonder what you think are the main barriers to a recalibration and reorganization of the radical Left. What are the traps or pitfalls that you see on the road ahead in the next few years as we reorient towards defeating resurgent fascisms and authoritarianisms? How can we aim higher and throw harder?

JR: The first thing I would say is that, while the rise of the far-right presents extremely acute challenges, and while on many levels it is true that we've been caught on the back foot, especially in the current electoral cycle, I do think that the Left is also growing, and

I also think we need to try to take the long view here. So when I talk about the Left's prospects, I am not just referring to the Left-wing candidacies that have come along within the most recent electoral cycle, but also to the social movements that have emerged in recent years and the rising political consciousness among a new generation of young people.

We millennials have been particularly hard hit by the consequences of the global financial crisis. Many young people are finding that there are awfully few possibilities for them to graduate into the type of comfortable middle-class life that their parents enjoyed. Of course, it's not just a middle-class problem; it's fundamentally a working-class problem. Many of us, myself included, are still very privileged despite these dreadful structural conditions. But by foreclosing home-ownership and stable employment—among other standard aspirations of the middle class—the crisis has upended one of the main stabilizing forces in capitalist class relations. Precariousness is on the rise, student debt is on the rise, housing prices are on the rise, and a lot of people are being priced out of the possibility to own or even rent a home. Young people's welfare expectations have been eviscerated in recent years. As a result, millennials are steadily becoming disillusioned with the political establishment and with capitalism more generally.

At the same time, especially in North America, there is a steady re-politicization of the question of race, and there have been tremendous mobilizations around extreme police violence and the brutality of state institutions against historically marginalized and oppressed social groups—including people of colour, immigrants and Indigenous people. On top of that you get this extreme wage stagnation over the past 30 or 40 years, you get gentrification and displacement and the disastrous consequences of the subprime mortgage crisis, and you see that as a result many historically marginalized communities are further pushed towards the sidelines of society, leaving large swathes of the population far worse off than they were before the crisis.

There are, of course, many more examples that I could mention here, but the bottom line is that all of this is generating a groundswell of social discontent in Western societies. The question is: who is going to be capable of working actively within local communities and within the workplaces to channel that growing discontent into a socially transformative or at least politically progressive direction? Clearly this is the Left's job. But at this stage, it is the right that has succeeded in capitalizing on the crisis. Its narrative is extremely simple: it just hammers home a racist message that has no basis in fact, but that is extremely difficult to counter in the absence of a real Left alternative. The keyword, I believe, is control. What the right claims to offer is to "take back control"—of our borders, our communities, our societies, etc. It's an entirely perverted and essentially racist and patriarchal message. But it seems to succeed in filling the vacuum left by the Left, which once promised to "take back control" over money, finance, production, etc.

So I believe that those of us in movements and on the Left need to think very hard about how to construct a type of common political project that can really start to "take back control" over the political economy, and challenge the right's—I wouldn't say monopoly, but it is almost a hegemony—on the representation of social discontent. Crucially, we should not give the right even an inch on racism and sexism: we should avoid the trap of social chauvinism at all costs. It doesn't work. You cannot out-compete the right on the right, and you don't compromise with racism and sexism. But there are many disaffected people who are not fascists and who may still be mobilized to enthusiastically support a progressive anti-establishment platform. Some well-intentioned comrades think they have already found the right formula: just get the latest socialist candidate elected and we'll be fine. But I'm afraid the challenge is a bit bigger than that. We actually need to develop much more inclusive forms of social and political organization that are capable of carrying forward a transformative political project through a combination of sustained popular participation and unrelenting pressure from below.

Luckily, we have a variety of traditions that we can build on in this respect. There's a long history of class struggle that has gone before us that we can take lessons and inspiration from. But there are also negative lessons to be learned if we are to avert the pitfalls of 20th-century socialism, both in its authoritarian and in its social-democratic forms. Our main challenge at this point, in my view, is to develop a type of political project that doesn't get hung up on the electoral cycle and that doesn't narrowly limit its political ambitions to the winning of state power, but that actually tries to do those things while at the same time developing a real popular movement. What we need are much more broad-based popular organizations through which we can begin to rebuild the Left's collective power—in a way that can really begin to challenge the dominant power structures in capitalist society, especially international finance and big business, which are at the root of many of the crises we face.

That's still a relatively abstract story at this point, but to make it more concrete, just look at what's been happening in the latest electoral cycle with the rise of a bunch of "old white men" as the representatives of a "new Left." Guys like Bernie Sanders in the US, Jeremy Corbyn in the UK, and Mélenchon in France embody a hope among many young people who have been squeezed hard in the crisis that perhaps in the next electoral cycle, if we are strong enough and manage to throw our weight behind these democratic socialist candidates, we will be able to unseat the neoliberals and the fascists alike. I see this approach as worth pursuing but fundamentally limited in the sense that it's far too focused on a small number of individual characters, and not focused enough on the construction of a broader form of social power.

Obviously Bernie would have won if Hillary didn't stand in the way—and the world would have been a much better place for it. And obviously we should prefer Corbyn or Mélenchon over May or Macron any time of day. The problem is that, if any of these old white dudes is going to be in office in the absence of powerful social movements able to radicalize the demands that are made upon them, and upon the political system more generally, it's going to be very easy for them to become swallowed in the trappings of bureaucratic state administration and blocked by what the French call the *mur d'argent*—the wall of money—that finance can unleash whenever a Left government pursues policies that it perceives to be against its interests. The structural power of capital can inflict an enormous amount of pain on any Left-wing government through divestment, capital flight, by refusing to buy government bonds, etc. This is not to say that we shouldn't try; it just means that we'll need a heck of a lot more than just the right guy in the Oval Office. We need to build up our collective capacities and learn to "strike at the helm."

That connects back to the story we discussed with respect to Syriza and the Greek experience earlier, which is that a Left alternative that is not supported by powerful mobilizations from below, that does not inspire active popular participation in the political process, that fails to carry forward a vision of how to radically transform and subvert the existing power structures within capitalist society and the global political economy more generally, is going to find itself relatively powerless in the standoff against financial capital and the establishment media, and ultimately against the far-right—which will benefit from the Left's failure and defeat, just as it now does from its relative absence. It is not a coincidence that we got to this point: we got here because the Left was defeated once before. You cannot undo this defeat with the same strategies that produced the defeat in the first place. We really need some creative new approaches on the Left.

The challenge moving forward, in my view, is to think in these terms: how do we begin to shape a real, broad-based, mass popular movement that can build inclusive and democratic expressions of social power without being narrowly focused on the electoral cycle; one that recognizes the importance of grassroots mobilization; one that is committed to a fundamental transformation of existing power relations? You cannot just talk about income distribution or job opportunities without acknowledging the underlying power structures that gave rise to these issues. You cannot just talk about imposing limits on international trade or international finance without recognizing that the trade liberalization and financial deregulation of the past decades has been carried out under the aegis of an incredibly powerful business class, one that has managed to pursue its own interests as part of a very successful but increasingly fragile political project that we've come to know as neoliberalism.

So when I speak of a political project I do not just mean the creation of a new party, or a candidacy to win the next elections. Yes, we'll need new parties. And yes, we need to win elections. But the key challenge, as I see it, is to think about what replaces 20th-century socialism in our times, as both a credible alternative to the far-right's monopolization of social discontent, and a transformative political force capable of moving beyond the endless succession of crises wrought by the neoliberal centre. That will require a degree of social organization far exceeding anything we have accomplished so far. It is only with the re-composition of the Left as a socially inclusive and radically democratic class project that we will begin to see this type of change—and we don't really have that much time left to get it off the ground. It's become a cliché to point it out, but it's true: the future of humanity depends on it.

CHAPTER SEVEN

Beyond a common dispossession: Deepening transnational anti-colonial and anti-capitalist solidarities

An interview with Glen Coulthard

GLEN COULTHARD is a member of the Yellowknives Dene First Nation and an associate professor in the First Nations and Indigenous Studies Program and the Department of Political Science at the University of British Colombia. Glen has written and published numerous articles and chapters in the areas of Indigenous thought and politics, contemporary political theory, and radical social and political thought. He lives in Vancouver, Coast Salish Territories. Glen's book, *Red Skin, White Masks: Rejecting the Colonial Politics of Recognition* (University of Minnesota Press), was released in August 2014 to critical acclaim. Alex Khasnabish interviewed Glen in February, 2016.

ALEX KHASNABISH: Can you tell me about the birth of your radical consciousness? More specifically, can you pinpoint an experience or a set of conditions, a text or a relationship that first sparked your radical imagination?

GLEN COULTHARD: I wasn't always an academic and the radicalization of my thought precedes me going to university. It probably goes back to the 1990s when I was working with one of your other contributors, John Munro, at this bookstore in Vancouver. John was always an avid reader and very critical about what he took on in terms of his reading habits. I remember one day he gave me a book that he had ordered; it was *The Wretched of the Earth* by Frantz Fanon. I tried to choke back that book that evening, but I didn't have a clue what was going on in it. I was never really a good student prior to deciding to go to university, but that friendship with John really cultivated an interest in a different set of literature. So my radical imagination began with me reading anti-colonial and Indigenous thinkers, and dabbling in Marxist and anarchist thought.

Then I decided to try going to school and took some Indigenous Studies courses at Langara, a community college on Musqueam territory here in Vancouver. One was with an important Indigenous feminist activist-scholar here in the city, Faye Blaney. That really set me off on a path of exploring anti-colonial literature and scholarship, specifically in an Indigenous context. The grades that I got at Langara allowed me to apply to the University of Alberta where I furthered my studies, now explicitly tackling these issues of settler colonialism and decolonization from a radical political Indigenous perspective, which by that time I was mixing more thoroughly with political theory.

By the time I was writing my PhD and doing research on the Dene nation's struggle in the 1970s, I'd come full circle, back to those sessions where we'd be sitting in John's shitty apartment commenting on the three volumes of *Capital*, or when I was struggling with Fanon and Sartre. In those days, in the mid 1990s, I had no idea that I would go on to be a professor. We were making minimum wage. I was partying too hard, living a really unhealthy life. By the time I was at the University of Toronto and then the University of Victoria working on my PhD, all of a sudden these literatures that I had read in the 1990s were central to every thought and every word that I was writing. It's humorous to me that I've come entirely full circle: from reading Fanon, drinking beers in John's living room, to reading Fanon, still drinking beers in John's living room, but now writing a book about it.

AK: Would you say that, in those pre-university years, you were cultivating an awareness in other ways, beyond reading and conversation? I'm thinking here about the forms of radicalism that emerge from land-based struggles and relationships that you write about in your book *Red Skin, White Masks*.

GC: That's a tough one, but I think no. But that's because of my own personal experience with colonialism and racism. I'd moved from Dene territory to the Westbank First Nation in Okanagan territory when I was quite young. That was a very alienating experience. Kelowna, the largest city in the region, has a very deep-seated conservative streak to it, and a lot of anti-Native sentiment. A lot of what brought me to Fanon in my current work was how much I identified with the impact that internalized colonialism can have on people. One of Fanon's insights is that the first response to that impact is a form of self-annihilation, an attempt to escape the difference that the dominant society represents as so repugnant. That was my experience in high school: always trying to escape this Nativeness that clung to me. I actively avoided engagement with Indigenous community or being scripted into that place in the world.

A self-transformation started to happen when these contradictions could no longer be smoothed over. I am Indigenous. People will always look at me and see me this way and again, in a very Fanonian narrative, I started asserting myself as such. That self-transformation meant a re-integration into community, purposefully on my part, and a relearning of our history, a re-learning of the value of our traditions. But at the time, when I was undergoing that process, it was still only a very cognitive process. It was still based in what I could learn by reading, by going through the archive, by talking to my family. It didn't involve that embodied, land-based aspect.

That only came much later, in the early 2000s, when I came to the realization that I will never understand this Indigenous history and theory that I'd immersed myself in because it's based on a practical ethics. Practice informs our critical and theoretical notions of colonialism and decolonization. And without engaging in those practices—the repetition of those practices and everything associated with that being in relationship to land—I would never get to that ethical core, the normative framework guiding Dene critiques of capitalism and colonialism. So that's when I started making an effort to learn from the bottom up by actually doing it, by engaging those practices with community members on the land. I'm still in that learning process. That's what I mean in *Red Skin, White Masks* by "grounded normativity." It's not an abstraction; it's not a normative frame that's abstracted out of place. It's informed by those place-based practices, but it's not bound by them. It's radically expansive.

AK: Was there a paradigm-shifting moment for you after you became a thinker, writer, and organizer, something that caused you to reconsider or recalibrate your commitments or ideas around social justice, radical social transformation and decolonization. If so, how?

GC: When I was doing my master's thesis at the University of Victoria in the Indigenous Governance Program, I was working within what had yet to become known as a "resurgence" paradigm, which was really militant in its Nativeness. Anything that I saw as tainted by the white man or colonialism, I inherently rejected. Again, this is a Fanonian story: Fanon refers to it as a vomiting-up of these values, a radical turn towards tradition and a revaluation of the practices that constitute it. So I wouldn't engage with any conversations with non-Indigenous perspectives or literatures; or, if I did engage it, it was from a dismissive stance.

But when I started doing the research on my own community's struggle, in the 1970s in particular, I realized it was very expansive. Their approach was born of an international, anti-imperialist conversation that was happening literally between Dene activists and people in Tanzania, as part of the phenomenon of decolonization that shook the post-war world. I found a couple of correspondences between the Dene nation and what they referred to as field workers, who were essentially embedded youth; militant community research sort of activists. The literature that the Tanzanians were drawing on a lot of the time was from the American Indian and the Red Power Movements in the US. And the Dene field workers were going to go over to Tanzania to learn their form of socialist, post-colonial development. They approached learning from other traditions and struggles from a Dene perspective.

That discovery re-oriented my work because now I didn't have to be worried about my work being "Native enough." I was approaching political theory and other people's struggles as a Dene person—from a Dene cultural basis—but in a way that allowed me to learn from and engage with those ideas. So my approach to political theory really changed from my 20s into my 30s, and I'm fairly flexible in what I'm able to engage with as a scholar and as an activist today. Unlike many scholars, I'm fairly non-dogmatic about the literatures that I draw from, but it's because I'm drawing from those literatures from a cultural base from which I transform and modify them, as you see with both Marx and Fanon in my work.

AK: What sorts of lessons do you think that experience offers activists and scholar activists today?

GC: It definitely calls for a position that is non-sectarian and anti-puritanical. I'm committed to an understanding of social change that is radically diverse, that is open to ideas, and that is grounded in our own community practices and cultural frameworks. I've learned a lot of this from Indigenous traditions but also to a certain extent from autonomist and from anarchist traditions. It's about relationships between paradigms rather than hegemonic struggles over some sort of unity. I think it would be great for everyone to be a bit more open minded when we discuss tactics or theory: by any means necessary and by any ideas necessary. We should draw on a diversity of perspectives when formulating our critiques, as well as when thinking about what alternatives might look like.

I'm not going to say I'm a non-sectarian; I don't find very much use in a lot of literatures or perspectives. But on ones where affinities can be more easily seen or drawn across diverse traditions, I think we should be more open than we've tended to be.

I was a rabid anti-Marxist when I wrote my master's thesis, but I learned a shit-ton when I abandoned that approach. It's one of the best and most sophisticated critiques of capitalist exploitation that we have. And it was stupid of me to position myself against it just because Marx was a white man. That work allowed me to see the intricacies of arguments that were really important to my commitment to a radical Indigenous nationalism. It led me to learn about how Marx himself had matured in his thought throughout his life to a degree where it was no longer in striking contrast to anarchists like Peter Kropotkin. That was a really important transformation in my radical thinking to be able to draw on these diverse resources from a Dene perspective in order to make sense of my world, in order to bust open my ideological space to think about what alternatives might look like.

AK: Was there a particular experience that allowed you to shift your perspective in that way?

GC: There were a couple of key experiences. One was my disdain for the education that I was receiving at the University of Toronto. There were some good people there, but generally it was a conservative, neoliberal experience. Marx was really the only critical thinker that I was reading in political science there, so he became one weapon I could have in my arsenal of argumentation that had to be contended with. And so I took the time to learn it. I convinced myself that if I was going to learn all these white folks, I was going to do it in as committed a fashion as possible because, as an Indigenous scholar doing the work that I do, I have to know my own voice and my own community's perspectives, but I also have to know, very thoroughly, the perspectives of our adversaries.

The other experience that was important to me was becoming very immersed in Fanon's work and his stretching of the Marxist tradition. It gave me insight into how one could engage theoretically with other traditions in a way that is informed by one's own experience of the world as a colonized subject. I have also always admired the spirit of the writing work of Howard Adams, the Métis Fanonian and Marxist scholar.

AK: To bring us to the present, do you think there are critical insights that Fanon's work offers to contemporary radicals who struggle for social change and social justice?

GC: I think one of the insights is how Fanon challenges the idea that all dialogue is fruitful. Fanon's characterization of the Manichean world of colonization is a really important formulation because, under the conditions of internalized violence and colonialism, the binary between self and other, colonizer and colonized, disappears: the native has been violently incorporated, in a structural but also in a symbolic way, into the colonial society. She sees herself as white, as settler, as in-sync with that world. The idea of a non-dialogical world without a distinction between friend and enemy, between colonizer and colonized, then emerges. The moment you understand yourself as on one side or the other is super crucial in developing a radical consciousness. Because then you can come to understand that your misery, your premature death, the destruction of your community, are actually the result of something outside of yourself; it's now a structural relationship. The narrative that colonialism propagates is that the violence that has been inflicted on you or your family or your community is because that's simply how you are: you're bad, you're evil, you're inherently violent, you're savage, all of these sorts of things. The break is in that moment of non-dialogue, that rupture of the dialectic that Fanon really affirms. It provides an alternative language to fight against the forces of accommodation, dialogue, inclusion, and reconciliation that are so dominant in the Canadian colonial narratives but also in places like Australia, New Zealand and, to a lesser extent, places like the United States. Rupturing contact is a really important moment, when you say, "I'm not going to talk to you. Our relationship is necessarily going to be one of struggle and conflict."

AK: What do you think Fanon's work offers activists, Indigenous and non-Indigenous, today in Justin Trudeau's Canada where there appears to have been at least a rhetorical shift in government and elite circles towards precisely these notes of reconciliation and dialogue, conveniently at precisely the moment when we are seeing such a militant Indigenous resurgence? And what are the limits of Fanon's perspective here and now?

GC: I part paths with Fanon on the construction of alternatives, and with the language of resurgence. It's been said that I do so too hastily, that I don't think Fanon has a valuable enough understanding of cultural politics as necessary for an alternative to colonialism. You can find some places in Fanon where he values tradition more than I lean on in my book *Red Skin, White Masks*, especially when you start looking at *Wretched of the Earth*. At the end of that book, he famously affirms Europe as morally bankrupt and demands that we, the colonized, the damned of the earth, don't mimic its atrocities in our own freedom struggles. So, assuming that we don't mimic Europe resurgence is necessarily going to have to be more grounded in experiences and cultural communities. That's there in Fanon. But Fanon also insisted that our decolonized futures are going to be born of the creation of our own values. That methodological commitment to self-affirmation, both collectively and individually, is what's crucial to me.

That's what I think people like Leanne Simpson have to offer when they say: "Look, we can use a host of resources when formulating our critiques and in condemning our colonial situation. But in the moment when we start to dream up alternatives, those are going to be born of our own intellectual systems, our own cultural frameworks, our own forms of thought, our own actions." So when I turn away from Fanon and towards folks like Leanne and towards Indigenous traditions, it's as much a methodological commitment to self-empowerment as it is a critique of Fanon. Unfortunately, my book has been interpreted the other way around as primarily a hasty critique of Fanon.

AK: Do you have concerns about the way some radicals turn toward others' traditions for inspiration? Especially in settler-colonial contexts, doesn't this desire to find paths towards alternatives in other ways of being also seem like an attempt to do an end-run around the deeply complicated work of dismantling the ways we live settler colonialism into being on a daily basis?

GC: There's the problem of appropriation, the desire to "go native," which has its own set of baggage that needs to be dealt with. But then there's the turn inward, the kind of care-for-the-self aspect that can really end up being its own form of navel-gazing, and it once again centres the settler subject, but now with this ostensibly radical narrative or turn. So how do you fight, on the one hand, the symbolic violence of appropriation and, on the other, the kind of psychological desire to Indigenize oneself and therefore legitimize oneself on this land? I think that that's where a lot of us are at in terms of the field of settler colonial studies. Initially, it was a transformative discourse where settlers could come to terms with being the problem. But in certain ways it has sedimented back into its own conservative, navel-gazing hegemony. How do we fight against that tendency? I think it's a relationship question. It's a treaty question; not a conventional treaty relationship between Indigenous nations and these big hegemonic institutions of the state and capital but relationships between peoples and communities. These would be relationships that could draw critical insights from each other's practices and traditions but based on relationality and autonomy. Non-Indigenous people have a lot within their own histories, traditions, and practices to discover that teach a different way, though many need to be modified too. For instance, there is a rich diversity within the anarchist or Marxist traditions. All sorts of subaltern knowledges have been stamped out through the hegemonic processes of neoliberal colonial capitalism. So it becomes important to re-build those practices, insights, and traditions so that we can come together and meet in a relationship, rather than trying to create a sameness through the appropriation model, and rather than turning entirely to oneself in the problematic naval-gazing settler-colonial sort of way.

AK: Does it ever make you worried or angry that your own work and commitments run the risk of being appropriated or fetishized by settler audiences? We've noticed that one of the responses to recent Indigenous resurgences and the public events we've organized around them has been a strange sort of penchant for settlers to have these public displays of emotion, these confessions of guilt and shame that don't seem to actually aim towards any substantive challenge to the settler-colonial system. What's behind that, and has it affected your approach?

GC: I'm not well-versed enough in the literature to give a thoroughly scholarly account of this, but it is what the effect of the Truth and Reconciliation Commission writ large has been. You have these big national events where Indigenous people are almost compelled to confess their pain, and then you have the cathartic settler breakdowns in response. The vital difference, though, is that the Indigenous subject has to live that violence over and over again in perpetuity, while the settler subject, relatively new to this, gets to have their catharsis and leave the stadium where these horrible narratives were expressed and pat themselves on the back because their work is done. They've identified with the victim and experienced a dulled down version of that pain. So it's like a confession: you go into the booth, express your sins, and, if anything, say 10 Hail Marys, and it's back to business as usual. So we need to fight against that kind of reconciliation and the sort of spectacles that enable a real sort of pacification, and also a fundamental misunderstanding of the relationship of violence that exists between Indigenous peoples and Canada.

The other question is of the fetishization of my own work. I'm actually surprised that the work has gained quite a bit of recognition from more critical non-Indigenous folks. I hoped that it would have been widely condemned. I should have a price on my head for writing that book. There's something weird going on there that I haven't totally put my finger on, and I'm definitely going to spice it up a bit when I start to get busy with writing my next book.

AK: We've certainly noticed this kind of fetishization and romanticization in our own context. Often, at social justice events, it takes the form of doing a perfunctory land acknowledgement at the beginning of an event and calling it a day, without any deeper consideration of the dramatic impacts of a decolonization agenda on our daily, lived experiences. But for us that opens into a broader question of what a decolonial politics would actually look like and feel like for settlers and what it would actually imply for our engagements with the state, with capitalism, with one another, with the land and so on.

GC: I have some students who are doing some pretty interesting work, following but also veering off from my work on the political import of negative emotions like resentment. In its nasty, Nietzschean form, resentment is fundamentally passive. It's reactionary, it's retrograde, it locks us into a weakened position in what Nietzsche refers to as a state of impotency, where we fail to act and only react, and in so doing privilege and centre the hostile world that we're claiming to critique. On the settler side of the equation, guilt and shame are emotions that similarly get characterized negatively. But it's really a matter of how those emotions are redirected because both guilt and shame can be passive in the negative, weak-kneed Nietzschean sense, but they could also be an important recognition of complicity in violence. And then, what are you going to do with it? It can spark that fire under your steps and create action. For Indigenous people, the question is: how do we hold each other to account and support each other in ways where resentment doesn't turn into an all-consuming form of self-destruction, but can be directed at the structures of the world that are fueling it. Similarly, for settlers, how do we stop that shame from internalizing itself into apathy or passivity, and turn it into direct action against the structures that are informing that shame? How do we develop an understanding of complicity and violence? And how do we do that across difference?

I think that shame can actually be important. And I think all of the literature on guilt is perhaps like the literature about anger and resentment. That's a little over-stated, perhaps; of course we need to troubleshoot how those emotions can collapse in on themselves and thus justify the status quo. But we also need to recognize their revolutionary potential and work to seize on that. It's pretty fucking useless talking to an unrepentant colonist; we've got a lot of them, and there's no room for dialogue, there's no room for movement. It's just a relationship of conflict and force. It is easier to speak to a repentant, shameful subject; they at least have some embodied sense that this isn't right, and that's an important self-realization to move in more transformative directions.

AK: What sorts of objective conditions of struggle would it take to move settlers from sympathy to action, and action that could drive the massive transformation of economics and everyday life that the politics of decolonization calls for? Will it take some sort of major crisis?

GC: I can just answer yes, it will be in moments of conflict and crisis. But, unlike narratives that see conflict and crisis as the constant structural future of colonialism or capitalism, I would actually emphasize the primary agency of Indigenous peoples who are constantly exposing those contradictions and provoking those crises, to which the state and capital have to react through forms of recognition or reconciliation. In the spirit of the autonomist Marxist tradition, I think that we are the central figurative agents here, and it's the structure of colonial capitalism that is constantly having to react to *us*, to the crises that our agency provokes through struggle, in an attempt to manage and pacify it.

Historically speaking, that's kind of what my whole book is about: how, from a colonial settler perspective, can the troubling radical agency of Indigenous peoples be contained, and what does that logic look like. What techniques of governmentality, to use Foucauldian language, must be employed in order to re-subjectify Indigenous subjects in ways that maintain the prevailing power relationships?

AK: In terms of visions for a different future beyond capitalism and settler colonialism, what do you make of the idea of the commons?

GC: Well, the commons stuff is interesting because it's held up amongst more radical folks as kind of sacrosanct. I joke that, in the anti-colonial and Marxist readings of John Locke's Second Treatise—which sets the philosophical and legal foundations for colonialism—the original sin is taken to be the moment of enclosure, when that which is common is turned into something private. But I actually think the original sin in Locke is the scriptural declaration that the world was actually given to man in common. That is the real beginning or impetus of Locke's colonialism: it renders the earth *tabula rasa*, free of other social and governing relations between people and place, relations that are not exclusionary but are, nonetheless, rule governed. There's a plurality of jurisdictions and social relationships that order the world, in which Indigenous or non-European peoples are central players. That complexity and plurality is erased by Locke and delegitimated by the colonialism his work empowered.

So when we think of reclaiming the commons, it can't be just in that *tabula rasa* sense, this sort of free-for-all claim to the earth and its resources. Instead, it has to respect and re-engage with those non-exclusionary forms, jurisdictions, and authority that govern the relationships between land and others. I think that Marx was on to this in his discussion of primitive accumulation. It's not just the rounding up and removing of people from all that they once had access to; it's also the entire wiping out of those social relationships that governed non-state, non-capitalist people, that governed their relationship to each other and to the land.

If we're talking about re-envisioning a world based on *that* understanding of the commons, then I am totally for it, and if that's what commoning means, then yes. But it's not just a battle of turf or resources that we no longer have access to because they've been enclosed or privatized; it's a battle to rebuild the customary social relationships and legal orders that existed before dispossession. We still tend to think too much in the Lockean sense of the private right to property and how it fuels the structures of accumulation. We don't talk enough about the other core ideological mechanism of dispossession that's rendering Indigenous people apolitical, as if they didn't have legal orders and social relations that governed the places that they lived and the people and the other-than-human others that were constituted within that legal order. So we have to focus, as Shiri Pasternak does, as much on jurisdiction and legal orders as we tend to focus on land and resources.

AK: In the absence of that, settler colonialism and capitalism seem very adept at coopting or marshalling the more limited notion of the commons to its purposes...

GC: Yeah. One of the more prominent early articulations of the commons was the sea. And it was necessary to have the sea or the ocean as common because you needed right of passage to colonize people. Some Indigenous Hawaiian scholars are doing some good genealogies of the ideas of the commons based on rich histories that point to how deeply implicated they are in colonial expansion and empire-building, particularly settler empire-building. This is not to throw out the idea of the commons completely, but it's not treating it as sacrosanct. The concept can have liberatory and emancipatory purchase, but it can't avoid its implication in and its reproduction of the colonial relationships of power, which are fundamentally dispossesive in their logic.

CHAPTER EIGHT

Radical internationalism: Race, colonialism, history

Isaac Saney

ISAAC SANEY is Director of the Transition Year Program at Dalhousie University, the groundbreaking program established in 1970 to redress the barriers and injustices that Mi'kmaq, other First Nations, and African Nova Scotian learners face when undertaking post-secondary education. His teaching and scholarship encompass Africa, Cuba, and Black Nova Scotian history. He is a long-time community activist and participant in the anti-war movement and anti-racist struggle, and is the co-chair and National Spokesperson of the Canadian Network on Cuba.

Trinidad

When I embarked on this introspective journey, one vivid moment remained—and remains—rooted in my memory. I was four or five years old, watching television at home in Trinidad. The 1939 RKO film *Gunga Din* (inspired by the 1892 poem of Rudyard Kipling, an arch-poet of imperialism) aired. Suddenly my father walked into the room, abruptly switched the television off, and declared, "We will not watch that blasted traitor to the people in this house!" This has resonated with me throughout my life. Gunga Din, Kipling's hero, identified more with the British who colonized India than with his own people, a conscious comprador agent of colonialism. Of course, at four or five years of age, I was unable to understand the sentiments and reasons behind my father's outburst. As I became aware of the epic anti-colonial, national liberation struggles, and then participated in the anti-apartheid movement, my father's remonstration remained my first inkling that other narratives existed beyond the dominant ones that suffuse and permeate society.

My years at Naparima College (junior and senior high school combined into one) in San Fernando, Trinidad's second largest city, introduced me to political discourse by various older students who were involved in workers' struggles and various Marxist study groups. This student engagement with radical alternatives occurred in a context directly shaped by the legacy of working class struggles of the 1960s and 1970s.

Particularly influential was the 1970 February Revolution (often referred to as the Black Power Uprising), which began as a rebellion of unemployed and alienated African youth and almost transformed into an actual workers' revolution when the urban working class (primarily of African descent) and the rural working class (predominantly East Indian) were on the verge of launching a united struggle. In response, the government declared a state of emergency and quashed the mass movement.

With revolution thwarted and the old order preserved, a period of intense reflection followed among progressive forces. Why was the revolutionary moment missed? Why had the opportunity slipped through their hands? Out of these discussions a variety of Left groups emerged, representing a range of tendencies, from pro-Moscow to Maoist and from Trotskyist to an armed guerrilla group. Intense debates and rancorous denunciations, of course, ensued between these various Left factions. Side by side with these ideological conflicts, a militant union movement—driven by the Oilfield Workers Trade Union and the All Trinidad Sugar Estates and Factory Workers—pursued state power through electoral means by launching the United Labour Front.

As the Cuban Revolution was both a Latin American *and* Caribbean revolution, it was often the touchstone for discussions about how to achieve a truly independent and just society, whose shared prosperity would be based on the socialization of Trinidad and Tobago's considerable oil wealth. In response, the ruling circles often invoked the fear that these various Left groups stood for the so-called "Cubanization" of the country. Fear transformed into hysteria with the advent of the Grenadian Revolution in 1983. With Trinidad separated by only 166 kilometers from Grenada, the fear of contagion was intense. Parallel to this ruling class dread was, of course, the Trinidadian Left's optimism that, if it could happen in "little" Grenada, then surely the progressive transformation of Trinidad was also a real possibility.

At Naparima College, I had two very contradictory but public immersions in political discourse. Every day, either in the morning or afternoon student assembly, the school principal would engage in an extended commentary on political and social life. We were spellbound by his sharp and pointed musings. However, his offerings were far from radical, amounting to an amalgam of social democratic and neoliberal nostrums. The power of his spell-weaving revolved around his rhetorical deftness, rather than the ideas presented. As a counter to his verbal deluge, I partook in self-organized lectures on a daily basis, during breaks between classes. I recall one particular older student (17 or 18 years old) who apparently was a member or at least a partisan of the Communist Party of Trinidad and Tobago. His themes encompassed anti-imperialism, socialism and a trenchant criticism of the Soviet Union.

What struck me most about my interactions with him was the zeal and deep commitment to a truly democratic and just society: I was struck by his conviction that the creation of such a society was not only possible but also inevitable. What stood out was the fervent belief that history's trajectory could be understood by human beings and this understanding could be used or harnessed by the exploited and oppressed in the struggle to overthrow an existing social order; *we could and would* shape society in the ways that would better serve the needs of the vast majority. The logic of history demanded the end of all forms of oppression and exploitation. In short, we were not chasing a dream, but were part of an ineluctable process leading to a new and better world. The comfort of this teleological schema lay in its affirmation that one was not struggling in vain.

While they formed the immediate local background for my introduction to politics in Trinidad and Tobago, these discussions and debates were beyond my comprehension at the time. I was too young, too naïve, and too ignorant to appreciate even the basic contours of the ideological-political-theoretical concepts the older student was introducing to me. But I once remember him saying, "Saney, one day you will understand all these things." I have no idea whether he still holds these positions as I have not been in contact with him since my school days. Nevertheless, he left an indelible impression.

My father's history also augmented my politicizing experiences at Naparima College. He was the head of medical operations at

Trinmar, the oil and gas exploration and drilling division of the state owned Petrotrin. Working very closely with the Oilfield Workers Trade Union (OWTU), the largest and most militant union in the English-speaking Caribbean, he had a crucial role in building and defending the most extensive health-care plan for workers in the country. Through his work, he garnered the reputation of someone who always stood-up for workers' rights in the face of management's efforts to undermine, what the union described as, their "precious medical plan." My father's collaboration with the OWTU allowed me to witness firsthand workers organizing for better working conditions and autonomy. His commitment to workers' well-being and frequent fights with management earned him deep respect and affection. He remains an exemplar of integrity.

Halifax

While I was introduced to radical politics in Trinidad, my own radical consciousness developed and was consolidated in Canada. My decision to study in Halifax was driven by both my goal of pursuing a university education and desire to understand my Nova Scotian roots. While I grew up with my parents in Trinidad and Tobago, my mother hailed from a small Black community in the Nova Scotia town of Amherst. Her family's presence in Canada or, rather, the territory that was to become Canada stretches back to the arrival of Black Loyalists. Black Loyalists were free men and women of African descent who came to Nova Scotia after the American war for independence. Many Black Loyalists were slaves who joined the British after being promised freedom, land, and economic security.

However, my first foray into activism in Canada was in the sphere of Caribbean politics. I joined the Caribbean Information Group (CIG), which operated on campus as primarily an educational organization informed by an anti-imperialist and pro-socialist outlook. My first major meaningful discussions about the Cuban Revolution, the failure of the Grenada Revolution, and the intersection of race, class, and gender occurred in the CIG. The CIG was part of a larger network of solidarity activism with the Sandinistas and in opposition to the Reagan administration's support for death squads in El Salvador and Guatemala. In the late 1980s, Halifax hosted major gatherings discussing Caribbean and Central American issues, attended by key figures such as Michael Manley, Cheddi Jagan, and Clive Thomas. CIG's strength lay in its commitment to an educational program aimed at making others aware of the reality of the Caribbean. It was during this time that I began to closely read history and political theory, especially numerous Marxist works. However, the group's failure to engage politically with Canadian society, either on Caribbean issues or on what was happening in Canada began to bother me. What was the point of all this understanding if we were not going to attempt to actively change the conditions we were critiquing, if not out right condemn them?! While not abandoning the CIG, I looked for other ways I could be directly involved.

Standing side-by-side with Central American and Caribbean progressive solidarity struggles was the anti-South African apartheid movement. In hindsight, my involvement in the Halifax Coalition Against Apartheid was seminal in my intellectual and political life. At the time I did not—and could not—recognize nor articulate effectively a key observation that influenced my political and theoretical development: the paternalist, nay, racist notion that western liberals and "leftists" had the right to dictate to the peoples of Africa, Asia, and Latin America the "proper" and "correct" ways to carry out liberation. This approach is informed by the presumption that the only valid and meaningful intellectual sources are Western-derived epistemologies and that there are no authentic intellectual traditions in the so-called "Third World." This racist, Eurocentric principle insists: we support your right to self-determination, so long as you self-determine in ways with which we are comfortable. Thus, support for national and social liberation struggles in the Global South was conditioned by ideas that westerners knew best how those struggles could be conducted.

Unfortunately, this racist outlook has infested too many Left formations. I remember being perturbed by the coalition's reluctance to endorse the African National Congress (ANC) or any other Southern African liberation movement. This reluctance, or in the case of some coalition members, open opposition, stemmed from the refusal to support armed struggle as a legitimate and necessary means by which to bring an end to the racist regime in South Africa. I also distinctly remember wearing a t-shirt emblazoned with pro-ANC and *Umkhonto we Sizwe* (the ANC's armed wing) slogans to a coalition meeting, which caused some discomfiture among the other attendees. As the 21st century careens onwards, this profound Eurocentrism that assumes appropriate struggles against imperialism can only dictated by the Western Left, and that the only intellectual reference points are from the West, continues as a pernicious disease. Perhaps this is epitomized by the World Socialist Website, the internet organ of the International Committee of the Fourth International (ICFI). It constantly adopts the position that the only viable intellectual emancipatory thinking comes from a very narrow selection of Western thinkers. No one who has theorized about colonialism, imperialism, and white supremacy are presented as offering anything worthwhile for consideration, indeed, they are disparaged. Race, for example, is merely epiphenomenal, requiring no special analysis.

During the 1980s to 1990s, a number of nation-wide Left groups operated in Halifax including the Communist Party of Canada (CPC), the Communist Party of Canada (Marxist-Leninist) (CPC(ML)), the International Socialists, and the Communist League. At one point they all tried to recruit me. At this time, I was quite active in the anti-war and Cuba solidarity movements leading me to work very closely with the CPC (ML) and the CPC.

While I was an active member of the Halifax Peace Coalition, my work in the peace/anti-war movement was primarily channeled through the No Harbour for War Collective, whose roots lie in the 1980s Halifax Committee Against Imperialist War. It provided a means by which to not only oppose war, but also to analyze its relationship with capitalism, and Canada's role within the Anglo-American system of imperialist states. The resort to war was not simply a policy choice of a particular government in power (inevitably and unavoidably the reigning executive of the capitalist class), but inherent in the very nature of monopoly capitalism. Even though the peace/anti-war movement might be able stop (however improbable that might seem) a particular war, to eliminate war as a threat to the world, imperialism itself had to be eliminated. In short, one could not have faith in the state or any political party that refused to recognize where the roots of war lay.

The No Harbour for War Collective continues to exist, challenging and refuting the myth that the Canadian state is and ever was a peacekeeper. It is a testament to the long peace/anti-war tradition in Halifax that while dormant for long periods, it often resurges. This is illustrated by large rallies against the first and second Gulf Wars, George W. Bush's visit, and in solidarity with Palestinians demonstrating against Israeli apartheid. Bush's December 1, 2004 visit represented a high-watermark of sorts when more than 7,000 people demonstrated, declaring that warmongers were not and still are not welcome in Halifax.

Shunpiking Magazine

Shunpiking Magazine, a small and modest attempt to challenge the media's monopoly on Nova Scotia's popular consciousness, was one of the most interesting and fulfilling projects I have been involved in. *Shunpiking* was conceived as a way to challenge Canada. The goal was to help develop independent media in Nova Scotia and to address problems and issues through "assisting the movement for progress [and] democratic empowerment."

As a member of the editorial collective—led by Tony Seed, the magazine's publisher—I found it exciting to regularly publish articles covering, among other things, the history of the Mi'kmaq nation, African Nova Scotians, Acadians, and workers' struggles in Nova Scotia. We conceived the *Shunpiking* project as "a counter to what we saw as the trivialization and marginalization of a people's history: reducing it to a few choice vignettes and events unconnected from the flow of real history."[1] At the centre of our conception was the principle that "people are the makers of their history and culture, not mere clay in the hands of 'systems' and their diplomaed historians and ideologists."

It was through my work at *Shunpiking* that I was able to explore in some depth the Black Nova Scotian experience, which was reflected in my academic writing and teaching. We underscored that Black Nova Scotian communities remained integral to the development of life and society of Nova Scotia through all of its historical twists and turns. The Black community remains a vital part of Nova Scotian and Canadian life. Not only does chronic unemployment and isolation suffered by African Nova Scotian communities continue but also, its historical experience is inseparable from the Nova Scotian tapestry. In the teeth of racism and provocations of every kind, aimed at placing and keeping them on society's margins, Black Nova Scotians built their own communities, forged long links, and sunk deep roots throughout Canadian society. This is exactly where Black communities can be found: not on society's margins, but operating as part and parcel of the everyday life of the wider community.

The historic significance of these contributions really stands out when the surrounding conditions are seen for what they were. African Nova Scotians are victims of colonialism. The presence of African Nova Scotians in that province is neither accidental nor purely conjectural. It is essential to note that Canada was a slave society until 1833. The significant contribution of Black labour to the economic development of Nova Scotia is ignored if not outright negated. The use of slave labour and the reduction of Black Loyalists and Black Refugee populations to a pool of cheap workers was crucial in building the infrastructure of this province. The existence of slavery established the precedent for exploiting African Nova Scotians as a readily available source of cheap labour.

This history profoundly shaped the trajectory of Black Nova Scotia. Some of the consequences include marginalization and disenfranchisement as evident by the Africville dispossession and the disparity of wealth and political power between social groups and classes. Throughout this history, the Canadian state was never a neutral actor or arbiter. It had very definite aims, as illustrated by the statements of Howe and Chamberlain, to create and reinforce the role of cheap labour and to ghettoize the community within the polity. This policy continues today.

The Black community has not remained passive, but has actively fought efforts to push and keep it at the margins of society. A poignant example is the founding of the African United Baptist Association (AUBA), an independent and community controlled organization. The AUBA became a key institution of Black Nova Scotian life, not only as a source of spiritual succor but also as the focus of educational, cultural, social, and political activities throughout all the Black communities. While formally a religious organization, the AUBA not only reflected Black social, economic, and political aspirations but actively defended and advanced the interests and rights of African Nova Scotians.

It is from this struggle to assert Black Nova Scotians' rights that the call and demand for reparations was raised. This demand exposes the unjust nature of the entire economic and political system. The victory of the Black community on the issue of reparations will be a victory for all. Black emancipation and the liberation of the entire society are inextricably bound together. The African Nova Scotian struggle for justice, equality, and self-determination demonstrates the capacity of all oppressed and exploited peoples to resist. Its potent legacy endures: People are the makers of history, not passive observers or powerless victims, but the active, conscious force in the fight for a better and just world.

Cuba

As an activist and academic, a significant part of my life is bound with Cuba. For more than 25 years I have been involved in the Canada-Cuba solidarity movement. The beginning of my involvement can be traced to the major international conference *Thirty Years of the Cuban Revolution: An Assessment*, held in Halifax from November 1-4, 1989. My discussions with Cuban officials and scholars from around the world gave me my first true concrete window on the Cuban Revolution.

I must be clear on this point: while today my activism and scholarship is dominated by Cuba and I hold a prominent position in the Canada-Cuba solidarity movement, my initial stance towards the Cuban Revolution was a mixture of ambivalence and skepticism. In leftist circles at that time, where you stood on the nature of the Cuban Revolution (akin to debate surrounding the Soviet Union) was a litmus test of your ideological, political, theoretical, and historical orientation. In 1989, I supported Cuba's right to self-determination, viewing the January 1, 1959 triumph of the liberation struggle led by Fidel Castro as an important blow against US imperialism. However, I did not consider Cuba to be a socialist society or even on the path toward socialism. What forced me to change my mind, and rid myself of rigid and dogmatic formulations about socialism was the collapse of the Eastern Bloc and the Soviet Union, and the subsequent survival of the Cuban Revolution. Why was the Cuban Revolution able to survive? Why didn't the Cuban revolutionary leadership simply capitulate and come to an agreement with US imperialism and surrender, as had happened in the former Soviet Union and the Eastern Bloc?

Cuba's incredible resilience led me to a serious revaluation of my previous positions, reinforcing the principle of "concrete analysis of concrete conditions." Or, to paraphrase the great anti-colonial leader and theorist Amilcar Cabral, that one should not "confuse the reality you live in with the ideas you have in your head." This new appreciation of the Cuban Revolution led to an increasing involvement with the Canada-Cuba solidarity movement, and a deep engagement with Cuban history and its own authentic and autochthonous political and philosophical traditions.

The significance of the Cuban Revolution extends beyond the geographical boundaries of Cuba. Since its inception, the Cuban Revolution has made an invaluable contribution to the global struggle for justice, social development, and human dignity. Cuba has established an unparalleled legacy of internationalism and humanitarianism, embodying the immortal words of José Martí: "Homeland is humanity. Humanity is homeland." In South Africa, for example, more than 2,000 Cubans gave their lives to defeat the racist apartheid regime. Today, the Cuban commitment to humanity is reflected in the tens of thousands of medical personnel and educators who serve across the world, battling in the trenches against disease and illiteracy.

On January 1, 1959, after a century-long struggle for national affirmation, liberation, and independence, Cuba embarked on a path that established authentic self-determination, placing the Cuban nation firmly in the hands of its people. In the 50 years that have passed, the Cuban people have resisted all attempts to take away their independence and freedom, and to re-impose foreign domination. They have repelled the unceasing, all-sided military, economic, financial, and propagandistic assault by the US, which has never accepted the verdict of the Cuban people.

It bears noting that any country trying to cope with and overcome the current worldwide economic crisis in a manner that favours its people, not global monopolies, is no small feat. This is all the more true for a country such as Cuba that has been subjected to a brutal, all-sided economic war from the US. Cuba's efforts in this regard are reflected in the latest United Nation's Human Development Report. In this annual report, recognized as the most comprehensive and extensive determination of the well-being of the world's peoples, Cuba is ranked with "very high development." In short, Cuba is a country that effectively uses its very modest resources for the benefit of its citizens.

Cuba is often described as the only foreign country to have gone to Africa and left with nothing but the coffins of its sons and daughters who died in the struggles to liberate Africa. Cuba illustrates the division between those who fight for the cause of freedom, liberation, and justice to repel invaders and colonialists, and those who fight against just causes, who wage war to occupy, colonize, and oppress. The island's internationalist missions in Africa and across the Global South are a profound challenge to those who argue that relations among the world's nations and peoples are—and can only be—determined by self-interest, and the pursuit of power and wealth. Cuba exemplifies that it is possible to build relations based on genuine solidarity and social love, and serves as an alternative that permits people to realize their deepest aspirations, and that another world is possible.

Conclusion: Reflections of a historian

The 21st century has become a distressingly painful journey for humanity, marked by an assault by the ruling circles on rights that were won through intense struggles waged by oppressed peoples and workers; a concerted campaign to eliminate their potent legacy and lessons. A critical aspect of these legacies and lessons is the recognition that accounts have to be rendered and settled with the past, that fundamental norms of justice and morality require redress of historical wrongs. In short, as William Faulkner once wrote: "The past is never dead. It's not even past."

As a historian, it seems bizarre to me that it is frequently necessary to affirm that the present is shaped by the past and that it is impossible to understand the contemporary world without explicating what has happened before. While the planet is beset with problems and challenges that are in many ways unique to the present phase of global historical development, this period cannot be detached from the past.

The present and ever-onrushing future are rooted in and bear undeniable historical birthmarks and stains of what has gone before. While this may seem a simple truism, a self-evident truth that requires no repetition, it is precisely this stance that is under attack. There is an orchestrated effort to paint the 21st century, particularly the process of "globalization," as a complete break from all that has happened before. "Globalization" is not only portrayed as inevitable and ineluctable, but as a fundamental rupture with the past; a rupture so profound and definitive that it has led to the assumption that history is irrelevant and useless to understand the onrushing future. History has lost value.

However, the study of history is not valueless or dead. The presentation and rendering of history is critical to the search for solutions to the problems that confront the world. What is at stake is the imperative to maintain an organized collective memory. We do need to break with the past and create a new basis for society by establishing new arrangements commensurate with modern times but we can only accomplish this by understanding the past. To paraphrase Marx, new struggles cannot draw their poetry exclusively from the past, but also from the terrain of the emerging future. New struggles cannot begin before they have stripped off all superstition in regard to the past.

My own work and reflections confirm the incredible capacity of all oppressed and exploited peoples to resist. Their potent legacy endures. They are at the centre of history, the principal active agents of their own liberation. This agency has embodied more than physical and armed acts of resistance. They are also the intellectual authors of their own emancipatory projects. Of course, people of flesh and blood make history, but never under conditions of their own choosing, and always within conditions transmitted from the past. Nevertheless, people are the makers of history not passive observers or powerless victims, but the active, conscious force in the fight for a better and just world.

Notes

1. http://www.shunpiking.org/bhs/our-philo.htm.

CHAPTER NINE

Truths my teachers told me: Circulating the histories of our movements

John Munro

JOHN MUNRO teaches US and international history in the History Department at St. Mary's University in Halifax, Canada. His publications include *The Anticolonial Front: The African American Freedom Struggle and Global Decolonization* (2017) and articles in the *Canadian Review of American Studies*, *Third World Quarterly*, *History Workshop Journal*, and in *Decolonization and the Cold War: Negotiating Independence*, edited by Leslie James and Elisabeth Leake.

I will confess a feeling of awkwardness and embarrassment. Although I aspire to have one, I'm not sure that I possess a radical imagination, especially in comparison to the other contributors in this collection. But my aspiration can hopefully be aided by taking stock of some of the ideas, events, books, and people that have helped shape my intellectual and political formation so far. In the spirit of historians Antoinette Burton and Dane Kennedy's observation that "historians produce situated knowledge, conditional on a variety of factors—including the untold or unacknowledged experience of historians themselves," what I want to do here is reflect on some of my experiences, and thus consider the development of my political consciousness alongside some people in whose company I'm honoured to be.[1]

My family immigrated to Vancouver from Glasgow when I was six. Our connection to Canada was an imperial one, slotted as we were into long established patterns of metropolitan migration to the British empire in general and the settler colonies in particular.[2] As representatives of the white Scottish working class, my family was exploited by capitalism, at times experienced real material deprivation, and on occasion felt emotional isolation in leaving the place from which we came. But we were also ensconced in colonial and racial privileges, not least our sense of entitlement in moving uninvited to the territory of someone else (that of the Tsleil-Waututh and Squamish Nations, in our case), and our insulation from having to think about the relationship between our racial well-being and the oppression of people of colour.[3] In addition, we were comforted in inhabiting an apparently default, generic, and unmarked racial identity. We were the beneficiaries of historical constructions which, as Cedric Robinson so memorably put it, "portrayed the whites as the forever normal, forever real, the race responsible for the order of the world, the race which was the destiny of the species, the true Subject of world history and its civilizations."[4] I grew up in a family that was able to avail itself, in short, of what historian David Roediger, following W.E.B. Du Bois, has called the "wages of whiteness."[5] These intersecting economic, racial, and colonial dynamics have shaped who I am in ways I'm still trying to figure out.

But the capitalism part made more sense to me first. My parents, like most people of their generation from the UK who were not destined for college for reasons of income and culture, did not finish high school. My father was an ironworker and my mother did retail and office work. Though I was neither intellectually nor politically precocious, as a teenager I could already see that their treatment was something short of fair. They worked hard but each year, if they were lucky, they'd be in the same place as the last. When I was in high school, after my dad endured a severe back injury at work, we were compelled to move from our modest apartment into public housing. Such experiences, combined with my mother's fondness for citing the social justice themes of the novels of Charles Dickens, helped me to better see that what capitalism promised and what it delivered were two quite different things. Doing for me in the late 1980s what he's done for so many others before and since, it was Karl Marx who really helped me move from a feeling about injustice to an analysis of social structures after a twelfth grade history teacher, Mr. Lefroy, assigned excerpts of *The Communist Manifesto*.

Here, it might seem, is the story of how my radical consciousness was born, against a world historical backdrop of Beijing, Berlin, and Baghdad as the Cold War ended and the New World Order began. But it's not. And that is largely because of race and gender. By the time I was in my late teens I had become convinced of the self-evident failings and injustices of the capitalist economic system, but I had thought little about being a straight, white man or the injustices others different from me faced. How whiteness granted my parents access to jobs that structural racism shut people of colour out of, for example, was not a line of thinking I had pursued. Herein lay two related problems, the first of which was giving only perfunctory thought to white supremacy and heteropatriarchy. The second problem was perhaps even worse: I thought that my consciousness *was* radical and that I saw things for what they were, rather than how they were presented through screens of ideology that skewed everything in favour of those with property. I rendered myself inattentive to radical possibility through the mediocrity of my own interpretation.

My parents, uncles and aunts, and other members of my family and community taught me more than they probably realized in their advocacy of labour unions (especially during the years of British Columbia's Solidarity Coalition, when the province teetered on the edge of a general strike),[6] their criticisms of those with too much, and their sense that relationships with people are more important in life than accumulating money. But still, as I finished high school, I wasn't able to figure out society and my location within it. I needed help. To my great good fortune, my future was to feature a long list of indescribably good teachers.

Not all of these teachers told me their names. In 1990, when I was 19, I spent much of my free time with friends, riding skateboards in downtown Vancouver. This was fun, but I also thought of skateboarding as rebellion and as a challenge to the institution of private property and the police officers and security guards who enforced it. The summer of 1990 was also that of "The Oka Crisis," the 78 day standoff between the Warrior Society of Kanehsatà:ke and thousands of Canadian police and military personnel later described by Mohawk anthropologist Audra Simpson as "a spectacular event that pronounced the structure of settler colonialism in Canada, illuminating its desire for land, its propensity to consume, and its indifference to life, to will, to what is considered sacred, binding, and fair."[7] Reading Simpson's powerful words now, I'm reminded of how little I understood of what was going on at the time. What I did learn was thanks to the individuals who set up a protest camp in front of the steps of the Vancouver Art Gallery, which was also a popular skateboarding spot. The police kept very obvious watch on the Art Gallery that summer, and they loomed threateningly when the city's official Health Officer reasoned that it had become necessary to destroy the camp in order to save it from an outbreak of spinal meningitis.[8] The protesters, some of whom I fell into conversation with during their several weeks there, taught me an embarrassingly obvious lesson that, enveloped in an "epistemology of ignorance," I had ignored.[9] It was those standing up to the forces of Canadian colonialism at Kanehsatà:ke and in solidarity actions like the one in Vancouver who really challenged power and who risked the violence of the security apparatus. Though I was slow to absorb them, two lessons shined through this experience: that my anti-capitalist skateboard rebellion was rather less subversive than I'd imagined, and that teachers and knowledge production are often to be found some distance from school grounds and campuses.

Nonetheless, formal educational settings and formal academic disciplines mattered. For me, that first meant Capilano College, where sociologist Noga Gayle's lectures pushed me to think more deeply about how capitalism is intertwined with other structures of inequality. Plus, Dr. Gayle assigned Noam Chomsky's *Necessary Illusions: Thought Control in Democratic Societies*, which was instrumental in systematizing my critique of the capitalist media and US foreign relations, especially at the moment when George H.W. Bush launched his invasion of Iraq. I went from Capilano College to Simon Fraser University, but worried about student loans and having very little idea about what graduate school was and how it worked, I did not complete a bachelor's degree. Instead, I drifted into years of office and warehouse work, interspersed with periods of unemployment.

Still, there were teachers. Like Brien Chomica, who I worked alongside in an office job and who taught me, among other things, about the political importance of sexuality and homophobia, not to mention what it might mean to live an examined life. A philosopher whose west end apartment featured walls lined with books, a framed portrait of Franz Liszt above the piano, and the likes of Vladimir Horowitz or the Red Army Choir on the record player, Brien guided me through what amounted to an extended, informal reading seminar. It was with him that I struggled through Plato's *Republic*, took in Hermann Hesse's *Glass Bead Game*, embarked on Theodor Adorno and Max Horkheimer's *Dialectic of Enlightenment*, and railed against Allan Bloom's *Closing of the American Mind*. Brien left Vancouver for Winnipeg in the mid-1990s, but his lesson that demanding books were worth reading beyond (as well as within) college campuses stayed with me.

During these same undisciplined years, I independently followed various circuitous trajectories initiated by Marx, Chomsky, and other thinkers whose names I first encountered in my initial and uncertain undergraduate years, like Michel Foucault and bell hooks. Intellectually, the mid-to-late 1990s were most memorably the years of *Capital*'s three volumes, Franz Kafka's *The Trial*, Emma Goldman's *Living My Life*, Antonio Gramsci's *Prison Notebooks*, C.L.R. James's *Black Jacobins*, Simone de Beauvoir's *The Second Sex*, Frantz Fanon's *Wretched of the Earth*, E.P. Thompson's *Making of the English Working Class*, *The Autobiography of Malcolm X*, Walter Rodney's *How Europe Underdeveloped Africa*, Michel Foucault's *Discipline and Punish*, Edward Said's *Orientalism*, Howard Zinn's *People's History of the United States*, Richard Drinnon's *Facing West*, Patricia Hill Collins's *Black Feminist Thought*, Edward Said's *Culture and Imperialism*, Howard Adams' *A Tortured People*, bell hooks' *Killing Rage*, Himani Bannerji's *Thinking Through*, and Ward Churchill's *A Little Matter of Genocide*. Many of the insights contained in such books, especially those pertaining to the relationship between race, gender, and culture, I grasped dimly at best, but around this time in my life people close to me, like Bethany Handfield, Anna Ruth, Katri Tahvanainen, J.P. Fulford, Glen Coulthard, and Amanda Dowling, also shared important lessons about feminist intimacies, ideological rigidity, and capitalism's colonial and gendered dimensions. Reading, I now know, rewards most when combined with reflective conversation.

By age 30, I was getting ready to grow up. After years of unsatisfying and underpaid work, I decided to go back to school to formally pursue my interest in ideas and politics, and perhaps even find my way to some sort of professional career. But just before I did came a pivotal volume. Stuart Hall's name had appeared in various things I'd read during the 1990s, but I didn't realize that his ideas were to be found in essays or on British television more than in single-authored books. So when I picked up a copy of *Stuart Hall: Critical Dialogues in Cultural Studies*, it seemed a curious mix of essays by Hall, interviews with him, and various other pieces about his ideas, about cultural studies, and about something called the CCCS.¹⁰ I simply worked my way from cover to cover in August of 2000, and was changed by the experience. Essentialism, articulation, and representation now occupied my mind's centre stage. After this book, I wanted to continue to think about capitalism and its critics, but no longer would I be able to bracket race while doing so. Although by this time somewhat prepared by previous encounters with anti-capitalist thought that foregrounded race, I found something in the clarity and eloquence of Hall's words that dug deeply into my consciousness. Marx looked different now, and that meant the world did too.

I returned to Simon Fraser University in the fall of 2000 to finally finish my BA and begin SFU's MA program in history the following year. This experience gave me the life-changing chance to study with three incredible mentors. In that first semester back into full time undergraduate study, I enrolled in a class on African American history with Karen Ferguson. With the help of fascinating lectures and assigned reading that included books like Ralph Ellison's *Invisible Man*, Elizabeth Clark-Lewis's *Living In, Living Out* and Manning Marable's *Race, Reform, and Rebellion*, I came to better understand how central white supremacy and African American history are to the United States, and how important the United States is to how the world works. I wanted to learn more.

The period in which I finished my BA and began my MA overlapped with distinguished novelist, poet, and public intellectual Dionne Brand's time as Ruth Wynn Woodward Chair in SFU's Department of Gender, Sexuality, and Women's Studies (then the Women's Studies Department). Through an undergraduate seminar and a subsequent directed readings course with Professor Brand, I learned more than I could have imagined. As we read, among others, Jamaica Kincaid's *Lucy*, Eden Robinson's *Monkey Beach*, Kerri Sakamoto's *The Electrical Field*, Jacqueline Jones's *Labor of Love, Labor of Sorrow*, Farah Jasmine Griffin's *"Who Set You Flowin'?"*, and most of Toni Morrison's oeuvre, I could more clearly see gender and sexuality as autonomous vectors of power in their interaction with race and class. I also came to more directly understand the quotidian operations of these structures and my place within them. As I slowly absorbed some of the implications of intersectionality, Dionne Brand's pedagogical brilliance and patience were instrumental to my progress.

That progress continued throughout the course of my MA under Karen Ferguson's supervision. It was here that I began to become professionalized, to become a historian. Academic disciplines, I learned as I tried to curb my idiosyncratic reading practice in order to write a thesis, were named such for good reason. During this period, I read many important books, and also got better at positioning them within fields of knowledge. W.E.B. Du Bois's *Black Reconstruction*, Richard Wright's *Native Son*, Ernesto Laclau and Chantal Mouffe's *Hegemony and Socialist Strategy*, Martin Duberman's *Paul Robeson*, Judith Butler's *Gender Trouble*, Robin Kelley's *Hammer and Hoe* and *Race Rebels*, Leslie Marmon Silko's *Almanac of the Dead*, Paul Gilroy's *Black Atlantic*, Arundhati Roy's *God Of Small Things*, Mark Solomon's *The Cry was Unity*, Winston James's *Holding Aloft the Banner of Ethiopia*, and with some foreshadowing, Cedric Robinson's *Black Marxism*, George Lipsitz's *Rainbow at Midnight*, Nelson Lichtenstein's *Walter Reuther*, Howard Winant's *The World Is a Ghetto*, and Alice O'Connor's *Poverty Knowledge* were among the landmark texts I enthusiastically digested at this point. All of them influenced me immensely.

It was also at this point that I met Jack O'Dell.[11] I first met Mr. O'Dell and began to become aware of his importance when Karen Ferguson invited him to join a few students who were reading Penny Von Eschen's influential *Race Against Empire: Black Americans and Anticolonialism, 1937-1957*. The book is exceedingly good, but Mr. O'Dell's perspicacity, wisdom, and grace are what stood out for me at this meeting. I became his research assistant a few months later, and over the course of countless hours sorting and cataloguing his papers and engaging in prolonged discussion, I became rich. Rich in new ideas, arguments, perspectives, and models of how one's life might be lived. Born in Detroit in 1923, Mr. O'Dell was an organizer, advisor, and movement intellectual in, to name just a few, the National Maritime Union, the Southern Christian Leadership Conference, People United to Save Humanity, and the National Committee for a Sane Nuclear Policy. He was also an associate editor at *Freedomways* magazine and Chair of the Pacifica Radio Foundation. In other words, Jack O'Dell could be found at the centre of many of the most important institutions of what historians have come to call "the long civil rights movement."[12] His articulation, in the face of countless encounters with racial capitalism's apparatuses of domination, of what historian Robin Kelley refers to as "freedom dreams" exemplifies the remarkable power that a radical imagination can wield.[13] With a generosity matched only by his brilliance, Mr. O'Dell, along with his historian and activist partner Jane Power, provided me with many lessons about the intricacies of oppression, the consequences of challenging power, and the long view of social movement struggle. At the same time, I was also being taught by activists in solidarity with the people of Iraq through sanctions and war about the myriad connections between international relations and nationally-structured oppressions. All of these teachers made it possible for me to go on to graduate school in history at the University of California at Santa Barbara.

I felt an acceleration of time at UCSB. Beginning in the fall of 2003, I lived in Santa Barbara for four years, then moved back to Vancouver to write and in 2009 finish my dissertation, which looked at African American anti-colonialism in the 1940s and 50s. At UCSB, there was so much to read and so many events to attend. What stands out? Some spectacular teachers and certain key books.

This round of teachers included the anti-war, labour, and immigrant movements that surged during the George W. Bush presidency. It also included fellow graduate students and friends who pushed me toward "looking beyond surface or easy answers and a desire to uncover the deep reasons for our present reality."[14] And it included mentors like Nelson Lichtenstein, George Lipsitz, Alice O'Connor, Cedric Robinson, and Howard Winant, who between writing prominent and widely discussed books made it a priority to make time to advise, push, instruct, and counsel me and other students on our road to becoming professional scholars. By this point, I knew to take in as much as I could of what these teachers had to offer. I also knew that it wouldn't be enough.

My teachers at UCSB also helped guide my reading. My interest in social movements and racial formation was only furthered by such watersheds as Michael Denning's *Cultural Front*, Clyde Woods's *Development Arrested*, Peter Linebaugh and Marcus Rediker's *Many-Headed Hydra*, Johnathan Lethem's *Fortress of Solitude*, Nikhil Pal Singh's *Black Is a Country*, Andrea Levy's *Small Island*, Barbara Ransby's *Ella Baker*, Zaragosa Vargas's *Labor Rights are Civil Rights*, James Smethurst's *Black Arts Movement*, Laura Pulido's *Black, Brown, Yellow, and Left*, and Nancy MacLean's *Freedom Is Not Enough*. Graduate school also provided opportunities to learn more systematically from Indigenous studies, with the help of Richard White's *Middle Ground*, Haunani-Kay Trask's *From a Native Daughter*, Lee Maracle's *I Am Woman*, Paul Chaat Smith and Robert Warrior's *Like a Hurricane*, Taiaiake Alfred's *Peace, Power,*

Righteousness, James Brooks' *Captives and Cousins*, Andrea Smith's *Conquest*, Ned Blackhawk's *Violence Over the Land*, and Pekka Hämäläinen's *Comanche Empire*. I began to try to square what these books had to teach about Indigeneity and colonialism with what I was learning about racial capitalism and social movements from Black studies and the literatures on social movements, though my efforts were halting here and trifling there.

In a development that was a bit surprising at the time but which makes more sense now, in graduate school I also began to feel the intellectual pull of diplomatic history. This was not the result of a sudden interest in the intricacies of how foreign policy is made, at least not within the terms of its self-understanding. Rather, it was books like Brenda Gayle Plummer's *Rising Wind*, Mary Dudziak's *Cold War Civil Rights*, Melani McAlister's *Epic Encounters*, Carol Anderson's *Eyes Off the Prize*, Elizabeth Borgwardt's *A New Deal for the World*, Victoria de Grazia's *Irresistible Empire*, Vijay Prashad's *Darker Nations*, and Glenda Gilmore's *Defying Dixie* that for me acted as a pivot between studies of culture, gender, empire, and racial formation on the one hand, and those of international diplomacy on the other. Across that pivot were diplomatic history books, such as Michael Hunt's *Ideology and U.S. Foreign Policy*, Odd Arne Westad's *Global Cold War*, and Walter Hixson's *Myth of American Diplomacy*. This reading trajectory was spurred on through my taking part, in the last months of grad school, in a summer institute put on by the Society for Historians of American Foreign Relations and expertly led by Fredrik Logevall and Jeremi Suri. Rather than a political digression, this intellectual rerouting was evidence of what historians call the "transnational turn," meaning that History (and other academic disciplines) are now less nationally bounded and more alive to international context. But in many ways this is a return to the position of earlier radical scholars, and for me a confirmation of what I had learned from Karl Marx, W.E.B. Du Bois, C.L.R. James, or Noam Chomsky, but with more of the cultural and gendered dimensions that Emma Goldman, Simone de Beauvoir, Patricia Hill Collins, or bell hooks might bring more fully into view.

I had learned three things by the time I got to my first academic job and moved to Halifax, at age 40. One was that I liked teaching, and the responsibility it brings in terms of sharing some of what I've learned and read with students. The second was that even if formally employed as a teacher, I'd always have much more to learn about injustice, exploitation, oppression, dehumanization, and of course opposition and resistance. Third, I knew I'd continue to make mistakes, get things wrong, and lack insight into my social location and the ways I continue to benefit from it. I agree with political theorist Alexis Shotwell, who writes that white people like me "don't just have a knowledge problem—we have a habit-of-being problem."[15] I don't see how it could be otherwise, though I also see how my very mode of articulation here may also confirm Sara Ahmed's point that "declaring one's whiteness, even as part of a project of social critique, can reproduce white privilege in ways that are 'unforeseen'."[16] Reading scholars such as Shotwell, Ahmed, and philosopher George Yancy, has been, to understate the case, very instructive.[17]

Today, I'm officially a historian of race, class, empire, and social movements in the United States and the world, but I'm really still a student of all those things. My luck in meeting excellent teachers, meanwhile, continues to hold. I have been living, after all, in the times of Occupy, Idle No More, Black Lives Matter, and the resistance to the Trump presidency and all it represents, and I have shared the city of Halifax with many people who have helped me to better understand history, oppression, resistance, privilege, power, and the relationships between culture and structure.[18] Parenting, I also now see, is among other things a new way of being a student, especially alongside my feminist partner, Jacqueline Maloney, and our children Clara and Roland. These lessons help guide how I continue to approach my work.

My scholarship and teaching explore some of the complexities of gendered racial capitalism and movements against it in the United States and the world in the 20th century. In particular, I am interested in how new kinds of knowledge and novel ways to imagine the world are produced in these encounters. Sometimes, I think, we wrongly see radical traditions as resisting injustice in a reactive way: the powerful exploit and oppress in their interests and the aggrieved react to the resulting hurts and horrors, while scholars theorize social relations and social movements take up those theories. What I have found in my research, and what I have learned in so many ways from all of my teachers in the overlapping domains of formal educational institutions and social movements is that our historical moment is shaped by structures of power and by the proactive ideas of radical traditions, and that sites located far from campuses and classrooms have often been the spaces in which new knowledge is generated.

My political consciousness is the product of a great many lessons, and as I've tried to gesture toward here, those lessons came to me courtesy of a remarkable roster of teachers. These teachers have taught me about the radical imagination, but perhaps most important, they have enabled me to assess the difference between approach and arrival. In my case, a white radical imagination is probably only achievable through a realization of its ultimate impossibility. Under the conditions of gendered racial capitalism, where, as per geographer Ruth Wilson Gilmore's compelling definition of racism, "state-sanctioned or extralegal production and exploitation of group-differentiated vulnerability to premature death" remains fundamental to the order of things, my claiming to be an ally or counting myself among the "good white people" seems a self-important distraction.[19] Instead, approaching the radical imagination—by supporting anti-racism, decolonization, queer liberation, and feminism while also remaining, as Stuart Hall rightly put it, "within shouting distance of Marxism"—without an expectation of arriving there, seems to be most in keeping with the truths my teachers told me.[20] But here I still am, writing about myself. Within that contradiction, of pursuing radical critique and thinking autobiographically while trying not to make myself the hero of my own analysis, lies embarrassment and awkwardness, but in this case also the great honour of getting to think about the radical imagination alongside the other writers in this collaborative publication.

Notes

1. Antoinette Burton and Dane Kennedy, "Introduction: The Autobiographical Pulse in British Imperial History," in *How Empire Shaped Us*, ed. Antoinette Burton and Dane Kennedy (New York: Bloomsbury, 2016), 2.

2. James Belich, *Replenishing the Earth; The Settler Revolution and the Rise of the Anglo-World, 1783-1939* (New York: Oxford University Press, 2009); T.M. Devine, *To the Ends of the Earth: Scotland's Global Diaspora, 1750-2010* (New York: Penguin, 2011); Bryan S. Glass and John M. Mackenzie, eds., *Scotland, Empire and Decolonisation in the Twentieth Century* (Manchester: Manchester University Press, 2015).

3. Robin DiAngelo, "White Fragility," *International Journal of Critical Pedagogy* 3, no. 3 (2011): 54-70.

4. Cedric J. Robinson, *Forgeries of Memory and Meaning: Blacks and the Regimes of Race in American Theater and Film before World War II* (Chapel Hill: University of North Carolina Press, 2007), 118. Historian Adele Perry's incisive reflections on growing up a settler in "Beautiful" British Columbia also speak eloquently to my own family experience: "Ours was a heavily astheticized vision of

place and space, one amenable to putting ourselves in the middle of, to making ourselves its subject, critics, and beneficiaries and always, the centre of its stories." Adele Perry, "Homes and Native Lands: Settler Colonialism, National Frames and the Remaking of History," in *How Empire Shaped Us*, ed. Burton and Kennedy, 152.

5. David Roediger, *The Wages of Whiteness: Race and the Making of the American Working Class* (1991; New York: Verso, 2007); W.E.B. Du Bois, *Black Reconstruction in America, 1860-1880* (1935; New York: Atheneum, 1962), especially 700. Readers might also take note of David Roediger's effective deployment of the autobiographical mode in the opening pages of his ground-breaking study.

6. On BC's Solidarity movement, see Bryan D. Palmer, *Solidarity: The Rise and Fall of an Opposition in British Columbia* (Vancouver: New Star Books, 1987).

7. Audra Simpson, *Mohawk Interruptus: Political Life Across the Borders of Settler States* (Durham: Duke University Press, 2014), 147.

8. Many of the activists involved in the solidarity protests were skeptical of this claim, and saw the Health Officer's pronouncements as in service of a political agenda. See "Infection Scare Ends Tent Protest," *Vancouver Sun*, 15 September 1990, A10.

9. Charles W. Mills, *The Racial Contract* (Ithaca: Cornell University Press, 1997), 17-19.

10. Kuan-Hsing Chen and David Morley, eds., *Stuart Hall: Critical Dialogues in Cultural Studies* (New York: Routledge, 1996).

11. For Jack O'Dell's activism and thought, see Nikhil Pal Singh's essential introduction and Jack O'Dell's essays in Nikhil Pal Singh, ed., *Climbin' Jacob's Ladder: The Black Freedom Movement Writings of Jack O'Dell* (Berkeley: University of California Press, 2010).

12. Nikhil Pal Singh, *Black Is a Country: Race and the Unfinished Struggle for Democracy* (Cambridge, MA: Harvard University Press, 2004); Jacqueline Dowd Hall, "The Long Civil Rights Movement and the Political Uses of the Past," *Journal of American History* 91, no. 4 (March 2005): 1233-1263.

13. Robin D.G. Kelley, *Freedom Dreams: The Black Radical Imagination* (Boston: Beacon Press, 2002). Appropriately enough, Jack O'Dell reviewed Kelley's inspiring and influential book shortly after its publication. See J.H. O'Dell, "Over the Rainbow," *New Labor Forum* 12, no. 1 (Spring 2003): 103.

14. Max Haiven and Alex Khasnabish, "What Is the Radical Imagination?" *Affinities* 4, no. 2 (2010): http://www.affinitiesjournal.org/index.php/affinities/article/view/70/187.

15. Alexis Shotwell, "Unforgetting as a Collective Tactic," in *White Self-Criticality Beyond Anti-Racism: How Does It Feel to Be a White Problem?* ed. George Yancy (New York: Lexington Books, 2015), 58.

16. Sara Ahmed, "Declarations of Whiteness: The Non-Performativity of Anti-Racism," *Borderlands* 3, no. 2 (2004): http://www.borderlands.net.au/vol3no2_2004/ahmed_declarations.htm.

17. George Yancy, "Un-Sutured," in *White Self-Criticality*, xi-xxvii. Also see Yancy's vital series of interviews on race with prominent philosophers in the *New York Times*: http://opinionator.blogs.nytimes.com/author/george-yancy/.

18. Thank you Phanuel Antwi, Afua Cooper, Chike Jeffers, Val Johnson, El Jones, Lynn Jones, Leigh Claire La Berge, Darryl Leroux, Radhika Natarajan, Sherry Pictou, Paddy Riley, Tina Roberts-Jeffers, Isaac Saney, and Ingrid Waldron!

19. Ruth Wilson Gilmore, *Golden Gulag: Prisons, Surplus Crisis, and Opposition in Globalizing California* (Berkeley: University of California Press, 2007), 28. My thinking here is also influenced by the varying perspectives found in Roxane Gay, "On Making Black Lives Matter," *Marie Claire* (11 June 2016): http://www.marieclaire.com/culture/a21423/roxane-gay-philando-castile-alton-sterling/; Brit Bennett, "I Don't Know What to Do with Good White People," *Jezebel* (17 December 2014): http://jezebel.com/i-dont-know-what-to-do-with-good-white-people-1671201391; Amie Newman, "'Good, White People' and Everyday Racism," *Medium* (12 January 2015): https://medium.com/@amienewman/im-the-good-white-person-and-i-need-to-fix-it-5d0364d46766#.kp7e06dyz; and Keeanga-Yamahtta Taylor, *From #BlackLivesMatter to Black Liberation* (Chicago: Haymarket Books, 2016), especially 191-219.

20. Stuart Hall, "Cultural Studies and Its Theoretical Legacies," in *Stuart Hall*, ed. Chen and Morley, 265.

CHAPTER TEN

Within, against, and beyond: Urgency and patience in queer and anti-capitalist struggles

An interview with Gary Kinsman

GARY KINSMAN is a queer liberation, anti-poverty, and anti-capitalist activist on Indigenous land. He is the author of *The Regulation of Desire: Homo and Hetero Sexualities*, co-author of *The Canadian War on Queers: National Security as Sexual Regulation* and editor of *Sociology for Changing the World* and most of *We Still Demand! Redefining Resistance in Sex and Gender Struggles*. He is a professor emeritus in the Sociology Department at Laurentian University, Sudbury. His website is: RadicalNoise.ca. Alex Khasnabish intereviewed Gary in August, 2015.

ALEX KHASNABISH: Can you pinpoint the moment of emergence of your radical imagination?

GARY KINSMAN: I think there are three moments. The initial moment of the radicalization of my imagination was quite cerebral. I grew up in a white middle class family in the 1970s. I was going to a public high school in Don Mills, Ontario—Indigenous land in the northern part of Turtle Island. I did well, but it did not meet my needs. I read a lot of Fidel Castro, I read a lot of Che Guevera, and I listened to Radio Havana Cuba. I remember also reading Daniel Cohn-Bendit's *Obsolete Communism, the Left-Wing Alternative* about

France in 1968. Those texts were an intellectual radicalization: they suggested things could be organized differently. One moment I remember is when the War Measures Act—essentially martial law—was announced in Canada in 1970 in response to the militant actions of the Front de Libération du Québec. My homeroom teacher at school asked us, "what do those people in Québec want?" and I was able to stand up and say something. I have no real idea what it was at that point in time—perhaps it was based on Radio Havana Cuba. After that, I got involved in the revolutionary Left and joined the Trotskyist movement.

I was a member of the Young Socialists and then the Revolutionary Marxist Group and the Revolutionary Workers League. While that was my first moment of radicalization it was also in some ways a straightjacket. I learned an awful lot from Leninist forms of organizing and from Trotskyism, but it was a very constrained politics; there was a certain type of correct line, and being closed to other possibilities. Partly because I was in the revolutionary Left I was placed in contact with the gay liberation movement; the Young Socialists at that time supported it. In August 1971 what's now called the "We Demand" demonstration took place: the first major gay rights demonstration in what is now called Canada (northern Turtle Island). I wasn't out then, but within a year I was experimenting with my sexuality, and another form of radicalism took place—one that had a much more embodied character to it—about sexuality, eroticism, and pleasure. I came out as queer and got involved in the gay liberation movement. This eventually became one of the points of rupture with Leninism, when the Revolutionary Workers League refused to integrate the lessons of lesbian and gay liberation and of feminism. They were unable to see these politics as pointing towards a broader revolutionary politics. That rupture opened up other possibilities for the radical imagination.

The third type of moment concerns the sorts of political practice that I was involved in. I remember when Toronto's York University Staff Association went on strike in the late 1970s. I was one of a whole bunch of students who went and occupied the president's office. It was a different sort of political experience because, as imperfect as it was, it was about direct action and direct democracy and it opened up new possibilities. Since then I've been involved in direct action-type politics within AIDS ACTION NOW!, the global justice movement, and anti-poverty organizing.

I see those three sorts of moments as transformative for my radical imagination: one very cerebral and intellectual, but leading to action and practice; the second being much more erotic and embodied; and the third actually being about the use of bodies to disrupt established institutional relations. All of these opened up other possibilities.

AK: Since those early days have there been other moments when your imagination or thinking changed significantly?

GK: There's a whole bunch, and they won't be in chronological order. I think the radical imagination can't be static or constant: it has to always be open to new voices, new struggles, and new experiences, because that's what is continually erupting around us. If you try to hold on to some sort of narrow truth or correct line, it actually works against your capacities to develop the radical imagination.

One of the major things that impacted me in the 1970s—especially after I came out in the context of the Leninist Left—was the feminist movement, which I found really transformative. It inspired in terms of how a politics can be organized differently and also in terms of challenging the forms of masculinity that I continued to practice even though I was a gay man. Some of that came to me from lesbian feminism but also feminism much more broadly. My rupture with Leninism, which occurred around the same time, came from learning that feminism and the insights of queer liberation couldn't really be integrated into the organization I was part of: actually existing Leninism would not learn from feminism and queer liberation. That was around the same time that Sheila Rowbotham, Hillary Wainright, and Lynne Segal's book *Beyond the Fragments* came out, and it suggested to me that there were other possibilities: prefigurative forms of politics and ways of organizing that were far more democratic, participatory, and open-ended.

This rupture with Leninism went further when I learned about the Zapatistas, autonomist Marxism, and John Holloway's work, which each talk about a very different way of moving forward in terms of how we theorize about the world. They insist that we refuse to give all the power to capital, which is unfortunately, I think, the habit of most mainstream forms of Marxism—including Marxist political economy—and even some currents within anarchism. We get constructed as victims, but if we actually see ourselves as the active agents of transformation and to some extent, as John

Holloway suggests, as the crisis of capitalism, it poses things in a very different way. Reading people like Harry Cleaver, Nick Dyer-Witherford, some of the autonomist Marxists' writings, and John Holloway, but then also seeing how they could relate to assembly-type forms of organizing, the Occupy movement, and various forms of organizing going on around me, has been a profound learning experience for me in both a cerebral sense and in terms of my organizing practices.

From the 1980s on I think the continuing challenges around racialization, Indigenous struggles, and anti-colonial struggles had a huge impact on me, which grew out of my engagements with feminism. There's a politics of solidarity and then there's transformative solidarity, where people get transformed by being in solidarity with the struggles of people of colour and Indigenous people. I think there's also the recognition of a certain politics of responsibility for people who are located in positions of relative social privilege. Obviously that privilege shifts and changes in people's lives according to a whole set of social relations: just because I am constructed as white by other people, and would construct myself as "white," doesn't mean it's the only thing going on in my life. But understanding that I was located within the social construction of whiteness placed some responsibility on me to challenge racism and racialization from that particular social location, which can open up space for people of colour and Indigenous people. So it's not a question of simply taking leadership or direction from people of colour and Indigenous people; it's also about recognizing that there's something specific about our role in struggles with other white people around racialization. I learned an incredible amount about the relationship between class and various forms of oppression from Dorothy Smith and George Smith, who I'll come back to in a moment, but also from Himani Bannerji. I think one of the most profound things I learned was from Himani Bannerji's book *Returning the Gaze*, where she basically says in response to white people saying, "Look, we understand your pain, we empathize with it," why don't you stop doing that? Why don't you start narrating your own stories about how you participate in this white normality and white hegemony without ever noticing it until a person of colour points it out to you? Why do you not start from your own vantage point to take this social relation apart? And that's really crucial. This mediational perspective, which is also a dialectical approach that she developed, actually moves us beyond this notion of intersectionality between discrete forms of exploitation and oppression. Rather, we see how various forms of oppression are simultaneously both autonomous and interconnected. You can think of class here and the way it is also made through relations of race, gender, sexuality, ability, age. This moves us beyond seeing them as entirely separate and distinct social relations. But to actually see them as always being mutually constructed and mediated in and through each other in a social and historical sense seems to me to allow us to understand that class never exists *without* these relations of oppression and that these relations of oppression never exist without class relations.

Obviously that doesn't resolve the question, and it's not a question of trying to get rid of the autonomy of these distinct forms of oppression. Bannerji uses Marx's notion of dialectical theorizing to allow us to see that every form of oppression and exploitation has its own specificity, its own autonomy: class is not race, it's not gender, it's not sexuality. They all have their distinct moments of specificity and have to be addressed autonomously. But that only gets you to a certain point, right? Because they are also everywhere made in and through each other in a concrete social and historical sense, we have to engage with that. This was a profound learning for me from my encounters with anti-racist practice and especially the work of Himani Bannerji.

The last thing I'll mention is my encounter, in academe, with the work of Dorothy Smith and George Smith. From them I learned about what is described as institutional ethnography—and from George Smith I learned about political activist ethnography. I found myself, as a graduate student in the early 1980s, wanting to do work that was useful for people in social movements, especially in queer-related social movements. In important ways, Dorothy Smith's work saved the day by providing me a way to link activism, organizing, and the movements I was engaged in outside the university with what I was actually doing in practice in the university, especially in terms of ethnography and taking institutional relations very seriously. But at the same time it allowed me to have a critical approach to institutional relations and resist participating in the institutionalization of movements and struggles. George Smith's work around political activist ethnography clarified that even more for me; it opened up the possibility not just that I could do work for oppressed people and even for social movements as an academic, but that my participation and activity in social movements, and everyone else's, could actually be profound pedagogical moments for the construction and transformation of knowledge. It revealed to me that social movements are already theorizing and engaging in research all the time, and that one could make this reality much more visible and critical.

You have to understand that one of the reasons why this made so much sense to me in the early 1980s, when I was a student at the Ontario Institute for Studies in Education, was that this was the time of the notorious and violent police raids of gay bathhouses in the city. I was in the group Gay Liberation Against the Right Everywhere and directly involved in the resistance to the bathhouse raids. This wasn't just an academic or cerebral experience: I was actually seeing how some of the notions I was learning in the university context were related to the political practice I was involved in. Up until that point I found the academic world littered with analysis of systems and institutions, these thing-like objects, but it was hard to understand how that analysis could help us transform the world. The ontological perspective that I learned from Dorothy Smith and George Smith made complete sense to me: the social world comes from social practice and from it alone—it comes from people's *doings*. *We* actually produce capitalism and *we* produce oppression. That ontological perspective can be quite horrifying when you realize that, at least in some ways, *we've* fucking done this to *ourselves*—though not under circumstances that we've fully defined or controlled. But the other side is that if we've done it to ourselves, if we've produced these relationships, we can actually fundamentally transform them. This type of ontological perspective has all sorts of permutations.

It's common on the Left to believe that capitalism, this external structure, is producing all these crises and problems in our lives, which can lead to the sentiment that "they should pay for it." It's a useful approach and I'm not putting it down entirely. But contrast that with what John Holloway says: "we are the crisis of capitalism." This means that while we bring these things upon ourselves it also provides a basis for a broader, more empowering critique. For example, workers produce surplus value for capital, but can also come to contest the ability of the capitalist to make profit, and thereby produce this crisis. In this sense it's about placing *us*—our own activity and agency—at the centre. Obviously that will vary in terms of different crises, there can't be a dogmatism to it, but it puts us in a different place and also poses very radical questions for us, frightening questions but also much more empowering and optimistic questions. I think this approach is really crucial for activism and organizing. It seems to me that, in contrast to ontologies that would give all power to capital or some social structure, this actually opens up—despite the moment of horror—a potential optimism, but not a naïve optimism. That rhetoric of "the system," which you hear littered all over social movement and Left organizing, is actually one of the things that prevent us from speaking to people. Some people may understand what a "system" is, but I'm not sure they want to understand the world that they live in as being like that. We need to think that through.

The other question is of epistemology, or theories of knowledge, which I learned to understand as this reflexive, mutually determined, and fully social notion of knowledge production. It's a really useful one. You and I are in relationship here, producing knowledge together in this very interview. For social movements and activists, it's tremendously useful to understand that this is what knowledge production is about. It has this fully social character: all of us know something, all of us can be theorists, all of us can be researchers, all of us can participate. Now, how you actually bring that about is much more difficult. It's more than just doing work *about*, and it's certainly more than just doing work *for*, although that has some usefulness to it. It's actually doing work *within* and *with*. It really poses as central the question of how you can get involved with movements and, perhaps in a broad sense, the Left. We're constantly doing research and learning things. How can we open that up?

You have to be constantly open to being challenged by new voices and new experiences. You need an approach that accounts for people who haven't spoken yet. This sort of dialogical approach is based on what the Zapatistas call a politics of listening and asking questions, not a politics of monologue or a politics of certainty. It's not compatible with the approach of some Leninists, anarchists, and other people too, that this or that person has the truth. That politics institutionalizes or freezes the radical imagination in particular and very limiting ways. You can still encounter people in the social movements of the Left who are basically repeating the same things they could have said 35 or 40 years ago as if nothing's really changed. But things have changed, in part through our own activity, practice, and resistance. Capital and the state have responded to our own organizing. Things are constantly in flux, and constantly changing.

AK: We seem to be at a moment right now where there's a resurgence of thinking that expresses real frustration with what's broadly been called "prefigurative politics" and exhorts us to get back to the "real business" of fighting the big fights—to the economic brass tacks of inequality. How do you make sense out of that? Is it people's impatience? Is it nostalgia for a moment when people imagine that the Left was more effective?

GK: I think that there's been a resurgence of the authoritarian Left in part as a result of frustrations with the anti-authoritarian Left, including that the latter isn't always great at organizing or at theorizing and strategizing. It's a critique we need to make of ourselves, but I don't think it necessarily leads to these conclusions. People fall back on how it's been done before, Mao did this or Lenin did that and it was supposedly successful, but of course I would actually ask a lot of questions about these "successes." What type of success are you talking about? And what ended up happening? If you want to talk about Mao, what actually happened in the Chinese Revolution that could have led to what exists now?

On the other hand, I think there's also a resurgence of certain readings of Marx's work, particularly political economy readings, that reassert the significance of the "economy." People forget that Marx's life's work, *Capital,* was actually entitled, "A critique of political economy." Even though there are some ambiguous formulations in Marx's work, by and large how I would understand it is that he was engaging in anti-economics: he actually wanted to talk about economics as a form of ideology that consistently produced the power of things and objects and hid the activities and agency of people themselves. The labour theory of value is actually a ripping apart of that reification of how capital supposedly produces new value. Marx shows us that it's living labour power—it's actual human beings and their activity—which produces the new value. So I read Marx as an anti-reification or anti-fetishism theorist *par excellence*. But unfortunately that's not how the bulk of people who would describe themselves as "Marxists" or part of the revolutionary Left read Marx. They read Marx as if his contribution is an economics or a science and they argue we need to get back to that, we need to get back to the forms of organizing that will allow us to put that into practice. This leads some people to Leninist notions that revolutionary consciousness has to be brought to the workers from outside their immediate and direct experience and into forms of organization which might not necessarily always be Leninist but that certainly reproduce top-down and power-over types of relationships to the working class. And then you get involved in what I would describe as a process of institutionalizing forms of struggle and organizing. Obviously unions have accomplished a great deal, but unions also have been very institutionalized just as political parties—including even the political parties of the revolutionary Left—get quite institutionalized.

So what do I mean by institutionalized? I guess here I could use women's studies as an example. It emerges initially as just part of the feminist movement: women who wanted to get together to talk about history, culture, and various things used university spaces to do so. But as women's studies gets taken up within the university context it also gets institutionalized. It gets separated systematically from its roots within grassroots feminist organizing. I'm not suggesting in any way, shape, or form that women's studies shouldn't exist, but I am talking about how that process of institutionalization was also an active process of ripping "women's studies," as it came to be called, out of the context of being an organic part of the feminist movement. So institutionalization is also how those institutions get taken up within state relations, legal relations, and regulatory relations, which transform them even if they started at the grassroots. Roxana Ng is really important here in terms of analyzing the transformation of grassroots community organizations into top-down organizations with particular types of organizational relations. You can specify this much more concretely in relation to seeking charitable status: if you want to get government funding, forms of regulation come with that. So there's this process of institutionalization that I think needs to be resisted.

At the very same time, we have to overcome some of the problems that have existed in parts of the Left where institutions just don't get taken seriously. Either from the position that we're completely outside these institutions and all we need to do is attack them, be against them, and have no relationship to struggling within them, or those who say that there's absolutely no realistic possibility of doing anything but working within them. And that comes back to Holloway's formulation of simultaneously acting *within, against,* and *beyond,* because that type of dialectical formulation is really crucial here. It's essential to take institutions seriously because those are some of the central nodes through which exploitation and oppression get organized in people's lives.

But it's also vital to recognize that they are not thing-like objects or systems external to us: we participate in helping to produce institutional relations. These institutional relations can have different characteristics but if we understand that we're within them I think some people draw the conclusion that we're just tainted by all of this horribleness. And of course we are. But if we understand ourselves as being within, this also gives us a sense of power because we produce these relations and we can potentially act to transform them and build something new in relation to the different types of institutional relations we're talking about.

So you have to be able to do research: you have to be able to produce knowledge. In some ways social movements are constantly doing this, like when we disrupt ruling or institutional relations, we can even think of this as a kind of political ethno-methodological breaching experiment. By disrupting those relations we learn how they're put together and about what is more effective in terms of a strategy to try to challenge them. So I think we actually have to take institutional relationships quite seriously because they're a central ground of struggle and they're also a central terrain on which we can win victories sometimes. Oftentimes it's by disruption and then understanding how disruptive direct action tactics might actually lead to people being able to get a social welfare check, something that social services claimed they would never get. That's been the experience of organizing in the Ontario Coalition Against Poverty, the Sudbury Coalition Against Poverty, and the Halifax Coalition Against Poverty. By understanding how these institutional relationships work you learn where to intervene effectively to get what you need, really quickly, which really helps people in their everyday lives and is related to building a much more dynamic, empowered movement against poverty or around other questions. Because it has a more direct connection to bodies and is participatory, direct action provides a possible basis for theorizing and doing research in a much more collective way.

AK: Critiques of spontaneity and calls for greater discipline and organization are ones we need to take seriously because they may point to where the anti-authoritarian Left has fallen down. Perhaps they also point to those areas or those people outside of our own circles that we don't speak or listen to enough. At the same time, it seems like such calls could also be politically nostalgic or, more troublingly, point to the resurgence of the tendency within some people and some organizations to attempt to assert their control over the direction of these struggles. How do you think about the question of organizing for radical social justice and social change?

GK: We need to figure out how we can organize much more systematically and in a more generalized way in terms of direct democracy or more radical forms of democracy. We need to understand that movements engage in a range of tactics and strategies, and this includes direct action. I think one of the most successful movements that we've seen over the last while is the Québec student movement of 2012. It was messy—nothing's perfect—but it was a movement with a solid anarcho-syndicalist type of organizing basis among students that had a protracted strategy, was engaged in involving the maximum number of people possible in direct democratic forms of organizing, and understood some of the contradictions and institutional relations it was up against. It was also able to become a mass movement. While the more established student federations in Québec ended up getting sucked back into processes of consultation and notions of partnership with the Parti Québécois government afterwards, the mass orientation of the Québec student movement actually showed us the possibilities of mass organizing on a basis that doesn't get sucked back in. On a basis, as well, that is not perfect because of course there were lots of problems around sexism and racism and other aspects of the organizing. Things weren't resolved but it still suggested an alternative way of moving that can't necessarily be reproduced in other places because of the unique features of the Québec student movement, which need to be understood. I think people have tried to replicate some of its features in what's often referred to as "English Canada," where student organizing is done in a very different way. Obviously there are very highly organized forms of practice that were engaged in the Québec student movement: it wasn't spontaneous at all, it was very organized but in a very different way than the top-down hierarchical forms of organizing. I think it's a good example of taking institutional relations seriously but not getting institutionalized in ways that would get sucked back into those ruling relationships.

AK: That example brings us back to the point you were making earlier: that in every moment of struggle and every moment of living you're encountering a field of social relations that are set against and shaped by context and circumstance. Coming back to this notion of Marx as a philosopher, as a social scientist committed to an anti-fetishistic approach, doesn't it resonate with an analysis of these moments not as things, not as singular entities, but actually as constellations of action, reaction, and of all this messy living that's going on as people are learning how to struggle?

GK: Yes, and the repercussions can be really long term. Maybe it would be useful to look at Syriza in Greece as a counter-example. Syriza lifted the hopes of large parts of the Left, especially those who hold out for some possibility that electoral parliamentary politics can actually lead to transformation. But what we see in the end is that despite the supposed radicalness of Syriza, because it never was able to *see beyond* in terms of its radical imagination— beyond the Euro-zone, beyond capitalist relations, and beyond existing state forms of organization—it could not conceive of a possible alternative except capitulation. And what it did not do was actually try to revitalize direct democracy and other forms of radical democracy, to actually proceed with the withering away of the state prior to any sort of fundamental social transformation. What I think you see there is that they end up only being *within*: the *against* gets lost, and there is no *beyond* in terms of their organizing.

It seems to me this *within, against*, and *beyond* with respect to institutional relations is absolutely crucial. It doesn't mean that they're always on the same level of importance, because obviously the concrete terrain of struggle shifts. But if you only focus on *within*—if it gets cut off from *against* and *beyond*—then there is nothing else beyond trying to reform these institutional relations. I've seen very well-intentioned anti-poverty activists who started off not being supporters of the Liberal Party in Ontario engaging in these endless rounds of conversation, consultation, and participation with the Liberal government around poverty reduction strategies, which lead to nothing except that the Liberal government can dress itself up and say, "we talked to all these people." It's about a certain notion of what is real and what is realistic: what is realistic is to be inside and to be within. But to not see ourselves as also being within is to not see where the struggle starts and also to not recognize the ways in which we've helped produce these sets of relationships and understand that we can actually organize differently to alter or get rid of these sets of relationships.

Against is absolutely crucial because it provides us with a direction of struggle. On the other hand, if you have an approach that simply says, "we're opposed to this and we're going to throw ourselves against this institution to try and break it," without any understanding of what's going on within it and that the struggle actually *starts within*, this can also be a problem. And then without having a notion of an alternative that we're building—that there's some sort of prefigurative dimensions or capacities to our struggle— that's also a problem. People who focus solely on *beyond* in the sense of alternatives might engage in little experiments, little collectives, and little experiences that are really important, but if they're not related back to *against* and *within*, there can be real problems. So it's this dialectical notion of how we can simultaneously hold in our practice and in our imaginations *within, against,* and *beyond*, along with the understanding that at some moments different aspects are going to be more important. I think that's really crucial in terms of how we confront institutional relations. I think it also poses some real problems for a lot of the struggles that we're engaged in, which are quite often defensive in the context of austerity and neoliberalism. So often we're just fighting to keep what was won by past movements; we're not actually struggling to alter the character of social services or whatever it is we're up against at that particular moment. We need to also see that the *against* and *beyond* are part of how we move from simply being defensive to actually having a more offensive, visionary, imaginative type of movement and organizing.

AK: Playing that *within* role inside of powerful institutions is awfully seductive, particularly for people whose paycheques and social status are tied to it. Are there lessons from your own experience that provide ways of fending that off? Not that *against* or *beyond* are easier to occupy as positions, but when you're within dominant institutions there also seems to be that constant risk of seduction. Are there things that movements and activists and organizers can do that you think are essential to fending that off? Is there something that we're missing here?

GK: Part of it is to actually have this discussion about trying to simultaneously be *within, against,* and *beyond*, which is not easy because it raises a whole set of contradictions and questions. If there was a basic agreement that those three moments were necessary to focus on, it would actually open up a different terrain of struggle. I think it's more about how we get to that point—how the anti-authoritarian Left can actually have a clearer understanding of it. Aspects of leftist movements certainly do: No One Is Illegal operates within, against, and beyond all the time. Perhaps with less development of the *beyond*, the anti-poverty activism of the Ontario Coalition Against Poverty does it. But there is still always a moment of *beyond* because central to many of their activities are free food and communal experiences that actually capture something that's *beyond* simply calling for raising the rates for social assistance.

I think another tendency of the more orthodox Left is to constantly look for examples around the world of a saviour. It was going to be Hugo Chávez, or Morales in Bolivia, or Syriza, or Podemos in Spain. Those are all really interesting experiences— I'm not trying to deny their significance—but they seem to be used to advance this notion that there needs to be some sort of leader, or there's some sort of top-down way of organizing that we have to get back to. In Greece this *within, against, and beyond* approach would have meant that from the moment of Syriza's election you would have been trying to build popular forms of power outside of existing forms of state organizing. You would have talked about alternatives, so that when the bailout referendum happened— which was actually an amazing result in terms of its rejection of the austerity consensus—it could have opened up so many other possibilities. But if you're only *within*, and you're not also *against* and *beyond*, there's nothing more you can do. While Syriza won the vote in the referendum, they were unable to pursue it since they could not see any alternative. It was almost that even though people voted against austerity it did not mean a thing. Basically it means that Syriza agrees with the Eurozone leadership that the referendum was meaningless because it was not realistic and not within the realm of possibilities. Crucial to developing a politics that's *within, against, and beyond* are notions of direct democracy— with all of the contradictions of assembly forms of organizing— and direct action. I don't mean a ritualistic notion that the only possible tactic you can engage in everywhere and always is direct action, but a notion of a politics of escalation and mobilization that includes direct action as part of it. Those are absolutely crucial.

For example, I went to a Black Lives Matter action that only had about 300 people at it but ended up blocking both lanes of the Allen Expressway in Toronto for two hours, which is quite significant, and people didn't seem to have a problem with doing this. So there may actually be a new openness, at least in some places, to that type of politics. Black Lives Matter demonstrations are really energetic and, in Toronto at least, it's a core of largely

Black women who animate and facilitate them; there's something interesting going on there. It seems to me that even though Black Lives Matter's official demands are about Special Investigations Unit investigations of police violence and these sorts of things, the character of the organizing actually points far beyond those demands, and I think that's really important. One of the interesting things about Black Lives Matter is that half of the people on the demonstration were people I would identify as being "white" and were there as allies who were quite willing to accept the leadership and direction of Black Lives Matter. For example, when the police came close, white people would surround the Black activists to provide some protection for them. So there are things about being an ally and the politics of transformative solidarity—perhaps a politics of responsibility—that are developing.

The other thing that's missing from a lot of our discussions is the significant labour involved in the reproduction of movements: who's doing this work and how little attention it gets? A lot of people get burned out, or feel like, "I've thrown myself against those institutions so many times and nothing's really changed, I just can't do it again." So we have to pause and think about this as a long-term struggle even though there are major flashpoints and moments of intensity. We have to figure out how to engage in a long-term struggle like the Zapatistas and, in some ways, the Québec student movement, which spent five years preparing for the strikes. We need that level of strategic perspective.

AK: It seems in the Global North right now, particularly on this side of the Atlantic, there are two timelines that are out of step. One is the eco-social crisis that seems to demand urgent action. The other has to do with the necessity of making time within our movements to deal with the important questions and dynamics you've raised. Are there ways of thinking about these timelines that allow us to address certain things urgently and yet do the kind of work that you seem to be suggesting needs to be done?

GK: Yes, somehow we have to figure out how to bring together urgency and patience or, perhaps more correctly, urgency and long-term organizing. The ecological crisis is absolutely urgent. And the crisis of state violence—police violence against Black people and Indigenous people in particular—is absolutely urgent. But we also have to recognize that if we want to change the world, and we're serious about that transformation, it can't happen overnight.

This is really unfortunate because the ecological crisis does pose major questions about whether we can actually get to *beyond*, and I think we have to notice that. I think there are forms of urgency that people get engaged in when they're directly impacted by something that needs to be respected. Folks engaged with Black Lives Matter are certainly going to prioritize that and justifiably be really pissed off at people who say, "all lives matter," which is completely dismissive and racist. The ecological movement is severely harmed by so much of it having been defined as *within* the status quo. So, for instance, we can't even conceive of things like campaigns against cars or collectively discussing why the tar sands still exist here. Those questions haven't even been posed.

Part of it is also the problem of the political perspectives that have dominated organizing. The climate justice movement is much weaker, at least within the Canadian settler state, than it is in Europe. Why haven't we been able to do much more? It was great that there were 6 to 10,000 people on the streets of Toronto for the March for Jobs, Justice, and the Climate, but it was just a symbolic march. It was on a Saturday afternoon; it didn't disrupt anything, didn't stop anything from happening. It could easily be ignored. It was good, but it wasn't really what was needed.

I want to come back to the experiences of people who say, "I've tried to do numerous things to change things and it never happens." Once I tried to get a student to go to a protest around tuition fees and they said, "I've been to five of those and nothing's changed. Why should I go to another one?" We have to recognize that that's not just about despair or apathy: there's actually something there that we could work with, that we could radicalize. It might be that those people are open to other forms of action. I'm also talking about the political depression that people experience. The sense that "we tried to change things for so many years and things haven't changed" needs to be politicized. This is all part of an approach that takes institutions very seriously but rejects institutionalization, combined with the method of *within, against,* and *beyond.* It shows us that this sense of urgency needs to be addressed by talking about what our alternatives are. How can we actually move from here to some other place?

AK: How do we know what institutions and institutional relations we ought simply to avoid? Are there some institutions and some forms of institutional practice or ways of relating that are so toxic and poisonous that they ought to be simply disavowed?

GK: First of all, to say that we need to be engaging with institutional relations is not at all the same as supporting them. We have to engage in struggle against a range of institutional relations. But I think you can actually distinguish between different types of institutional relations in terms of the way you fight against them. A much more direct and frontal opposition is necessary in relation to the police, the criminal justice system, the prison system, and the military because of the character of those sets of institutional relations. They're directly used against us and our struggles— although people still get taken up within them. For instance, because of the research I've done, and knowing a number of people who were directly affected by the national security campaigns against queers, I've been engaged in a struggle to try to get the Canadian government to issue a formal apology to queer people who were purged from the military and from the public service. It's not the typical politics I would be involved in and some of those people who were purged from the military still are quite supportive of it and its institutional relations, which of course is not my perspective at all. It's a first step in struggle but it can't stop there.

I also think it's there in terms of the law. Obviously the law is a terrain of struggle, and we have to engage with it, but we also have to recognize that it's not our terrain. To simply get taken up within the rule of law, which might restrict forms of arbitrary ruling power every once in a while, is not all of what we need. We need to move far beyond that, because those types of institutional relations are directly tied into colonialism and the manufacture of Canadian nationalism that are then utilized, for example, against Indigenous people. While this is something we need to oppose, it doesn't mean that we don't also need to understand how those institutional relations work. You actually need knowledge of them; you can't simply stand outside them and say from an external position, "we can just attack them." But there are other sites, right? I'll just mention a few. Within state relations, social services are delivered to people in horrible and disempowering ways—but they also are the result of people's struggles in the past. In very distorted ways they actually give people some of what they need. Of course, social service agencies do a lot of policing of people living in poverty. So it's not to say you should get sucked up within those institutional relations, but to recognize that they're part of a different terrain of struggle. Another would be the mainstream media. A lot of people are interested in social media and building alternative forms of media and I think that's all really good, but I think there are complexities around social media that need to be talked about in more detail. To simply write off mainstream media as being the enemy, which some people on the Left do, disavows how sometimes you can productively enter into media frames; it might not be the story you want to tell but it gets through to lots of other people. That's a different terrain of struggle, even though it's corporate controlled and, as a result, becoming much more difficult to have any sort of influence in the mainstream media. Again, we have to understand how those institutional relations work in very complex ways if we're going to be able to struggle against them but also intervene within them. Even if the terrain of struggle is direct action—disrupting those relationships—it means it's not the same as dealing with more directly disciplinary state institutions like the police. We need to move *within*, *against*, and *beyond* these terrains of struggle.

There are different types of institutional relations and there's also the question of social forms and state forms. It seems to me, in a general sense, that state forms and relations are on the other side. They're not on our side. We need to understand that. We will need to engage within them, organize alternatives, and try to transform them where we can. However, a politics of engagement with even the "less repressive" state forms and relations—if you want to use that expression, though there's a lot of repression even in "non-repressive" state relations—still means that we don't get taken up in that top-down, power-over, disempowering set of relationships. We also need to recognize that neoliberal capitalism and neoliberal rule use strategies of "consultation" and "participation, which sound so wonderful, but can be used nefariously. It's great to talk, it's great to participate, but these can ultimately be strategies that defeat us when they're not on our terms. We need to understand this as a pervasive social process and not as a matter of moralism that people talk about in terms of "co-optation"—as if somehow the individual wasn't strong enough or there's something wrong with them. Indigenous peoples' struggles must be put at the centre of a lot of this organizing, because if you centre Indigenous struggles and anti-colonial struggles, especially in settler-colonial contexts, it makes for a far more critical approach to even those supposedly less repressive aspects of state formation. The status quo is based on the colonization of Indigenous people, so to simply argue for getting some white middle class people to be part of it is a real problem. This is something that unfortunately happened with the gay liberation movement, which made remarkable progress and won amazing victories on the level of formal legal equality. In the end, though, it is about a layer of largely white middle-class gay men becoming part of the white middle class. It can't be totally reduced to that—there are obviously real impacts on people's lives—but it wasn't the people who waged the struggle in the streets who gained the most benefit. It was the stratum of white middle class professional managerial types who gained the most. So on the one hand that's a movement that people would cite as having won amazing victories, but it's produced a context in which queers of colour, queer working-class people, queer street people, lots of trans people, and lots of lesbians are simply not part of that elite— not part of that project of getting into the white middle class. I don't think it's a movement anymore but a nebulous "community" that has a certain type of class character to it.

AK: How do you think about critiques of what's been broadly labeled "identity politics," especially those from the avowedly radical Left? Does this debate have implications for your political thinking and action?

GK: I think it's important to note that there are different types of identity politics. Often times the identity politics that go unrecognized and unchallenged are those of the group in the centre—like the white middle class. On the Left you see it in the notion of "working class" as a group comprised mainly of white male workers rather than the autonomist Marxist notion of class as being about struggle and about unpaid, reproductive, and domestic labour as well. I think it's important for us to understand that when people are denied identities and identifications, they are going to demand them: they're going to search for them, and they're going to try and claim them. These demands are actually quite useful and important in struggling against oppression, as long as they don't become essentialized and as long as they maintain a connection with social and historical conditions and with class questions and struggles.

I think part of the problem around gay liberation was that it managed to get through a series of transformations entirely separated from working class experiences and class struggles. The movement and its successes became associated with a different type of class and class struggle: the white middle class and gaining access to it. So in a certain sense there's a one-sided class war that's gone on within gay communities that was never named as such. In general I think that identity is a problem, but I think we also have to recognize its complexities. This comes through in Himani Bannerji's work: if identity is understood in an anti-essentialist way as always being social and historical, always changing, and always related to class and class struggle, I think there are still ways in which it can be used. I am quite opposed to the way that some critiques of identity politics have been used against movements of oppressed people and I want to maintain that opposition. On the other hand I do think there's something about the way in which identity politics has been utilized to separate particular social movements against oppression from struggles against capitalist relations—class relations—that's actually allowed for middle class elites to emerge in various communities in ways that I think are quite troubling and need to be opposed.

AK: It seems to me, especially in the anglophone North Atlantic world, that there's an inability to speak convincingly outside of our own activist milieus—an inability to engage a bit more broadly, to speak to people who are not already convinced. Some of that has been built up around not just the question of how we identify struggle but also how we identify ourselves within our own radical spaces as "activists" versus "non-activist" people and the jargon that gets associated with that. Does this become a way of insulating ourselves from the messiness that you've been pointing to?

GK: Well, there are a couple of things here. One has to do with the isolation of the Left. That isolation comes from a whole series of developments: the McCarthyite witch-hunts in the US, the red-scare campaigns in Canada, campaigns of oppression against the Left, police infiltration of different groups, and more. Because of these things, some people on the radical Left are isolated but also come to isolate themselves. As a result, I think sometimes we forget that people's consciousness and practice are often quite contradictory. Someone could subscribe to capitalist beliefs one day and be on strike the next. There's rage and contradictory forms of resistance to capitalist and other oppressive relations even as these relations might not be understood as such. We have to tap into that; we have to find ways of speaking to that in a much more popular way and not just dismiss people as being apathetic or pro-capitalist. We need to understand that there are flashes and times of rebellion in lots of people's lives. The question is, how do we connect with that? How do we find languages for that? Part of it is to re-situate ourselves as being engaged in mass politics and often contradictory struggles. How do we relate to that experience of contradiction, that experience of rupture, that experience of rage which might have really messy aspects to it? How do we recognize that many people can be rebels so that we're not setting ourselves apart as some sort of isolated revolutionary elite with its own cliques and ways of doing things, perpetuating a sort of revolutionary purity? If it's not the revolutionary purity of Leninism it might be the revolutionary purity of how this tiny network of people operates. These little experiments could be really good but, again, they can become isolated fragments of *beyond* that aren't connected to broader struggles *against* or *within*. In making a mass anti-capitalist and anti-oppression politics, we need to connect with the everyday rebellions in people's lives. These moments of rupture and rebellion can open up more profound paths to social transformation and liberation through acting dialectically and reflexively *within*, *against,* and *beyond* capitalism and oppression.

Reading List

Bannerji, Himani. *Thinking Through: Essays on Feminism, Marxism and Anti-Racism*. Toronto: Women's Press, 1995.

Brock, Deborah. "'Workers of the World Caress': An Interview with Gary Kinsman on Gay and Lesbian Organizing in the 1970s Toronto Left." http://www.yorku.ca/lefthist/online/brock_kinsman.html

Cleaver, Harry. *Reading Capital Politically.* Oakland: AK Press/Anthesis, 2000.

———. "On Schoolwork and the Struggle Against it." 2006. http://la.utexas.edu/users/hcleaver/OnSchoolwork200606.pdf.

Cohn-Bendit, Daniel.*Obsolete Communism: The Left-Wing Alternative*. Oakland: AK Press, 2001.

Dean, Jodi. *Crowds and Party*. London: Verso, 2016.

Dyer-Witheford, Nick. *Cyber-Marx: Circuits and Cycles of Struggle in High Technology Capitalism*. Chicago: University of Illinois Press, 1999.

Federici, Silvia. *Revolution at Point Zero: Housework, Reproduction and Feminist Struggle*. Oakland: PM Press, 2012.

Haiven, Max and Alex Khasnabish. *The Radical Imagination: Social Movement Research in the Age of Austerity*. London: Zed Press, 2014.

Huot, John. "Autonomist Marxism and Workplace Organizing in Canada in the 1970s." *Upping the Anti* 18 (2016): 91-105. http://uppingtheanti.org/journal/article/18-autonomist-marxism.

Holloway, John. *How to Change the World Without Taking Power: The Meaning of Revolution Today*. London: Pluto Press, 2005.

———. *Crack Capitalism*. London: Pluto Press, 2010.

———. *In, Against, and Beyond Capitalism: The San Francisco Lectures*. Oakland: PM Press, 2016.

Kinsman, Gary. "The Politics of Revolution: Learning from Autonomous Marxism." *Upping the Anti* 1 (2006). http://uppingtheanti.org/journal/article/01-the-politics-of-revolution.

———. "Direct Action as Political Activist Ethnography: Activist Research in the Sudbury Coalition Against Poverty." In *Political Activist Ethnography: Studies in the Social Relations of Struggle*, edited by Ian Hussey and Laura Bisallion (forthcoming).

Kinsman, Gary and J. Charbonneau. "Beyond Waving the Red Flag: Towards a Political Critique of the Revolutionary Communist Party and the Revolutionary Student Movement." *Radical Noise* (2017). http://radicalnoise.ca/2017/05/24/beyond-waving-the-red-flag-towards-a-political-critique-of-the-revolutionary-communist-party-and-the-revolutionary-student-movement.

Ng, Roxana. *The Politics of Community Services: Immigrant Women, Class and State*. 2nd ed. Halifax: Fernwood, 1996.

Rowbotham, Sheila, Lynn Segal, and Hilary Wainwright. *Beyond the Fragments*. London: Merlin Press, 1979.

Smith, Dorothy, *Institutional Ethnography: A Sociology for People*. Lanham, NY: Alta Mira, 2005.

Smith, George. "Political Activist as Ethnographer" In *Sociology for Changing the World: Social Movements/Social Research*, edited by Caelie Frampton, Gary Kinsman, AK Thompson, and Kate Tilleczek, 44-70. Halifax: Fernwood, 2006).

CHAPTER ELEVEN

Be prepared to win: Indigenous struggles and the radical imagination

An interview with Sherry Pictou

SHERRY PICTOU is a Mi'kmaw woman from L'stikuk (Water Cuts Through High Rocks), Nova Scotia. She graduated with her PhD from Dalhousie University and has been recently appointed as an Assistant Professor in Women's Studies focusing on Indigenous feminism at Mount Saint Vincent University in Halifax, Nova Scotia. Her research interests are decolonization of treaty relations, women's role in food and lifeways in land based practices, and Indigenous refusal politics. Max Haiven interviewed Sherry in June, 2016.

MAX HAIVEN : You've said that the question of how you arrived at a radical consciousness is a difficult one for you. Why?

SHERRY PICTOU: It's such a difficult question for marginalized people because, from a very early age, I knew that something was different, that somehow we were different. I'm not sure how radical it was, but it was off the beaten path. I was brought up on a small reservation in the late 1960s where we had to attend a public school. From day one I knew something was very different. It was a horrible experience; nasty. I didn't know at the time it was racism, but I was conscious of somehow being different, and was always walking on eggshells. As soon as I left the reserve I knew I was in a different sphere, all of us kids knew that. The experience of school was counter to how I was raised with my grandmother and some of the older folks in the community. I was very conscious that we were Mi'kmaq, that there was something called treaties, and that we never signed over our land. As I went through school I really started to question why we were so different, compared to what the old people were telling me about our community. At the time we were also experiencing severe social problems with alcoholism and so forth.

My radical consciousness came into being when I realized there were outside forces influencing life on the reservation, which caused things like inadequate housing. Until I was 12 or 13, I was brought up without running water. I had to lug water and use outhouses. I experienced all sort of things. But when I was 19, I had my son. The sub-regional office of Indian Affairs used to be in downtown Halifax and at that time, Indian Affairs was downloading some services to band councils, but not all of the programs. There were certain things that you still had to go and apply for at the office, including sub-standard housing. I had a broken firebox in the woodstove and I had this baby boy, so I applied for a propane heater or something to help out but never got a response. To make a long story short, I ended up adopting us out to an extended family in Eskasoni and they ended up raising my son. But months later I directly inquired in person as to what happened to this request for this propane heater. Usually there was a Mi'kmaw social worker, at the office, but she was on leave and this non-Mi'kmaw woman in the office put all the blame on the Mi'kmaw woman. Later it was found out that there was some kind of office politics and she was trying to get this Mi'kmaw woman removed. As a consequence, my son and my case became involved in that process. That was probably a turning point for me, along with seeing the simultaneous situations in the community.

So it's hard for me to point out one particular point when this radical consciousness came. But I think after that experience and the experiences in my community, I started putting two and two together, and I started questioning everything, and have questioned everything since then.

MH: How did that lead you to the different forms of activism you've been engaged in since that time?

SP: Once I realized that there were outside influences on our community and others were experiencing them as well, I struggled to gain some type of insight. Those influences eventually led me to university as a mature student. The first thing I was trying to understand was where all that money from Indian Affairs was coming from—or not coming from—and why there was inadequate housing. I also wanted to know about how Indian Affairs was using audits to police the community's finances. So I took a correspondence course through Acadia University to understand these audits. Later, when I attended university, I majored in Political Science and Atlantic Canadian Studies and, bit-by-bit, it started coming together. I was exposed to the policies of the Federal and Provincial governments and began to understand why things were happening. I recognized that there was this contradiction between assimilative policies and segregationist policies. Residential schools are one example and the reserve system is another. I mean, when I was a child, non-natives weren't allowed on the reserve after sunset; this was part of the Indian Act which has since been changed, but it gives you a sense of that contradiction between assimilation and segregation.

I struggled through academia doing a Bachelor of Education. The experience took me back to grade four or five when I was in elementary school and had to learn about my people as savages. We weren't properly named and our history was misrepresented. During my BEd program we were made to take an education psychology course and it was my lowest mark. We read statistical analyses of the dropout rates and education indicators of people from lower socio-economic classes, and here I was in the class, someone who shouldn't have been there, studying this. So again, my experience was denied. But when I did my Master's I got to discover people like Paulo Friere, author of *Pedagogy of the Oppressed*, and Myles Horton, who founded the Highlander Center in Tennessee, and that's when the world started making sense to me. I thought, "Okay, it's alright to have an alternative point of view, it's alright to be who we are historically, traditionally," because I knew that there was this other, dominant reality that was being imposed on us.

I guess that's when I began struggling at all times to bring Indigenous reality to the forefront. It led me to sitting on the Band Council of my community, to eventually sitting as Chief, which was a paradox because then you're receiving federal funding that is tied up with all kinds of strings. I remember one time, in response to us refusing to follow a certain policy, Indian Affairs wanted to put our community under third party management, even though we hadn't even run a deficit. The trick has always been trying to maneuver around policies and finances to meet the real needs of your community. So I've always had that critical perspective, I've always tried to honour the ways people were evolving in my community, and their realities of hunting and fishing and so forth. We tried to establish programs that would honour that while navigating the bureaucracy.

And then the Marshall Decision came down in 1999, when the Canadian courts acknowledged our people's treaty rights to hunt and fish for a livelihood. I always say that fishing chose me, I didn't choose fishing. I say this because, for several years, fishing dominated the political agenda of organizations and our relationships with non-Indigenous fishermen. It was really difficult to explain to others how fishing was only one of many issues we were dealing with in our communities. That was a hard experience. It's still difficult for me to talk about because there were different political and economic realities that came out of the woodwork. But one thing that really came to light was the power of privatization and the corporate sector.

This of course led to my community joining the World Forum of Fisher Peoples in 2002. When we first read the preamble of the Forum's constitution, it described exactly what we were trying to do in that organization: create a sustainable livelihood rooted in our culture. From 2006-2014 I served as Co-Chair and during that time we advocated for international guidelines for the Rights of Small Scale Fisheries. This was passed at the United Nations in 2014. Canada became the only country to refuse to pass the guidelines until we managed to mobilize support here and from scholars around the world. We are now trying to ensure that we remain involved in how these guidelines are implemented.

MH: The struggle around the fisheries and treaty rights and oceans brings us to a theme we're exploring a lot in this book, which is the question of the commons as both an idea and a reality. I've really learned a lot from the work you and Martha Stiegman have done about the Mi'kmaq idea of *Netukulimk*.[1] Do you see that term as akin to the idea of the commons?

SP: This is something I've been contemplating. I'm also probably not pronouncing the word right; I've heard elders argue about how to pronounce it and there are varied interpretations. If you talk to some linguists they'll say it means just "making a livelihood" or "living off the land." And others have interpreted it as "taking no more than what you need." There are a lot of Indigenous concepts like that throughout Canada. And what they all indicate to me is a relationship with the natural environment, with the world around you.

Where commons becomes problematic... now, I have to back up a bit, because this is what was so scary about what happened to the fisheries. At one point, fisheries were considered a common resource. Now they've been privatized; those fish are starting to be owned, in a way. This happens time and time again, and I've been doing a lot of thinking about it. Commons becomes problematic when you even look at the word and its origin in modern times. It's juxtaposed against private property. It's one side of a binary. Here in Canada, reserve land is actually officially Crown Land, in other words land held in common by the Crown. It's so ironic and revealing that Stephen Harper, on his way out, passed bill C-48, which amended voting procedures in the Indian Act to enable the privatization of reserve land. But this is an old pattern, if the commons are in that binary with private property.

We've had learning circles with people from across Canada, particularly Indigenous people, trying to come up with a notion of commons. It's always been an aspirational notion I think, and in reality, today, I'm not sure if there's a difference between public property and the commons. That's where it becomes problematic. The non-Indigenous clam diggers on the Bay of Fundy have taught me a lot about this, because we have a lot in common with them. They're always being propositioned by the government to take a lease on the wild clam beds they harvest, so they can have private control over them. But a lot of them won't do it, first because they know that Bear River First Nation is nearby and we might have something to say about it, but second because they don't want to repeat the structure of owning a common resource as private property. They've seen how it works when a private company gets ownership of a beach and closes it off, so it's counterintuitive for them.

But there's a bigger problem too. You could have a little piece of property, even hold it as a commons. But if there's a big disaster like an oil spill that affects a large territory, that affects the groundwater, what's the good of the commons then? Bruce Kneen writes about this and he tries to come up with alternatives. The idea of common property must mean that private property exists, by contrast. And so what are you really transforming? That's not to take away from the work being done by people trying to coexist in common areas. However, you have to think about it. At first glance the commons is a really appealing concept, but when we look into it I'm not sure that we fully know what it means.

So I boil it down to this: what we need to do is to really explore what we mean by property, and what we really mean by a piece of land, whether it's common or private? Are we talking about owning nature again? Are we trying to own something, or should we be exploring our relationship to it? And that's where I think the resurgence of Indigenous perspectives is so important. It's very difficult for this resurgence to take place amidst neoliberalism and colonialism. But it means asking: what are the relationships between people and land? And I think Indigenous people and all people living on the northern part of Turtle Island can visit that. What is their relationship to the land? Once we explore that then perhaps we can move forward with what needs to happen. That's the short answer, but it's very complicated.

MH: One of the concerns we have, as people who've used the term commons a lot and have a real fidelity to it, but who are also settlers on Mi'kmaq lands, is that the idea of the commons might be a Eurocentric concept with colonial implications. There is this tendency among some scholars to make this easy equivalence between the worldviews and practices of the Western European peasants, from whom we derive the word "commons," and of Indigenous people. We are worried there's a kind of linguistic and conceptual colonialism going on that allows settlers to first of all lump all sorts of Indigenous people together and second to imagine that they can all be held within this idea of the commons that just doesn't fit. But then maybe there are other, older, grounded traditions or ideas, like *Netukulimk*, that we should be thinking through, concepts and practices that are Indigenous to these lands and these relationships.

SP: The idea of the commons is probably an attempt to try to understand a relationship to land. And as we well know, Marx himself, in his later writings, was starting to come to terms with this a bit. I think there's a danger in terms of trying to do this kind of categorization. What are you categorizing: Indigenous people, or the land? There's a danger in using the terminology of geopolitical borders or nation-states to describe Indigenous peoples for a number of reasons. And I think Canadians are now becoming aware of just how diverse Indigenous communities within Canada are. You have the Mi'kmaq and other Northeastern Woodland peoples, but then you start going to the prairies... the Blackfoot on the prairies think differently than the Haida on the coast, and that diversity in itself opens up an exploratory discussion of how those people lived in relation to those lands and ecosystems. Here in the Atlantic, there's some work that was done by Trudy Sable, Bernie Francis, and Roger Lewis that illuminates the traditional so-called hunting districts. They weren't boundaries per se, they were actually defined by river systems and all the relationships bound up in that.

I think the commons is a very Eurocentric notion, but it's difficult to find the language for how to discuss these concepts. I'm even becoming uncomfortable with using words like territory, sovereignty, ceded and unceded because it's the language of a legal jurisprudence of another culture. And sometimes we're forced into using that language. But it distracts us from the relational understandings we might have within those natural environments.

There's a great book that just came out by Eve Tuck and Marcia McKenzie, *Place in Research: Theory, Methodology, and Methods*. They centre Indigenous worldviews but within the context of environmental studies. I think that's a starting place, based on the question: what are our relationships? I think this work has already started and we're seeing more and more collaborative efforts between Indigenous and non-Indigenous peoples against the state, against corporations, against fracking, mining, and the fisheries. I think this is a good thing, though there are problems in the dynamics of those types of coalitions and a lot of dangers for social movements and struggles in terms of who controls or directs them, and whose interest they serve. But I think there are excellent examples of coming-together around what people will tolerate in terms of what's happening to the land.

Hopefully that will be a start. Once we can determine what our relationship is to the lands, to the waters, then we can figure out some ways that we can—I don't even want to use the word coexist but, can exist, all of us, in a way that protects those lands and waters, in a way that sustains life. I know that sounds a little bit sensationalized, but unless we understand those relations I don't think we're going to be able to move forward. We will always be faced with this form of neoliberalism that's undermining the essence of life through pollution and the exploitation of natural resources.

MH: That brings me to my final question, regarding those coalitions and the horizon of struggles today. What does it mean to win? My experience and the research we've done with the Radical Imagination Project has revealed a lot of different approaches to Indigenous and non-Indigenous solidarity, but often the potential or vision seems hazy. If we want to overcome the neoliberal death-system, does that look like all of us building some kind of common future together through shared governance? On the other hand, there are Indigenous activists who are thinking more in terms of parallel sovereign systems, that settlers will have their governance, Indigenous people will have their governance, and they'll have to come together on some level. Or, is it about creating some kind of shared umbrella of common governance? Or can we even answer those questions?

SP: It's a very difficult question. Sometimes we get caught up in our struggles with a linguistic problem in terms of what terminology to use. Sometimes I wonder about using terms like sovereignty, and a lot of times I find that, even with the best-intentioned alliances and coalitions, you start talking about ownership.

And again, this is where we need to explore our relational understandings: what does it mean to own something? It's a very difficult problem. I'm not saying it's impossible.

I'm having trouble with the idea of parallel governance, or coexistence. For my little community for instance, that's impossible. If you were to take a closer look at it, we're not all Indigenous. There are a lot of intertribal, inter-racial relationships. At what point do you cross, do you inter-communicate?

We're locked in the same notion as before: there's the commons, and then there's private property. But if you start looking at the relations, there would be another notion of the different nations living side-by-side. If you look at a city like Toronto you can see a lot of communities and peoples living side-by-side. But I think we have to explore those relational understandings before we can even start creating that.

I was talking to a colleague of mine about a problem that I've always had with terms like colonialism, post-colonialism, decolonization, anti-colonialism: what does that all mean? And what are you decolonizing towards? In post-colonialism, what constituted "post" and so forth? I'm working it out, but I really, firmly believe that we still need to decolonize to get to the space that we can create or recreate an alternative. And I'm not sure if we can create that alternative while we're still colonized.

I look at the treaties, and at the different interpretations of those treaties. Obviously it's the Canadian legal interpretation that dominates, but if you look at some of this work that's being done that examines what the original Indigenous signatories thought about those treaties you see that, again, it comes to this relational understanding. So to renew those treaties we need to renew those relational understandings, and I think that's what we have to figure out: at what point do we come together? Or do you make a utopian group living over here, and another group living over there, and you never come together? I think that's impossible. I know that some of the more resurgent, militant Indigenous thinkers would probably think differently.

But let me put it this way: I used to ask the Chiefs what would happen if the government, all of the sudden, said to us "all right you have your treaty rights. You can implement them." What would that mean? And I think the harsh reality about the Marshall Decision was that we did not have a concrete alternative. Again, there were misunderstandings about what we were even trying to achieve with that court case. They always say: be careful of what you ask for, you'll get it. And if you get it, then what do you do, you know? A typical example was with the New Democratic Party government we had here in Nova Scotia. I don't think they knew what to do, and they took ill advice, and the neoliberals got in.

When you win, be prepared to win. I think this is why radical imagination is so important. You need those spaces to create something you're prepared to step in with. If not, the powers-that-be will find a way to undermine your victory.

Notes

1. "Netuklimuk [is a] concept central to Mi'kmaq culture and worldview that 'every living and non-living object was created equally, including humans. Everything in life in inter-connected. To sustain life in a respectful manner, lives must be lived responsibly and with consideration'" (230). Martha Stiegman and Sherry Pictou, "How Do You Say Netuklimuk in English? Learning through Video in Bear River First Nation," in *Learning from the Ground up: Global Perspectives on Social Movements and Knowledge Production*, ed. Aziz Choudry and Dip Kapoor (London and New York: Palgrave MacMillan, 2010), 227–242.

Subscribe online at uppingtheanti.org

1 year $23.50
(US $34)

2 years $40
(US $62)

UPPING THE ANTI
a journal of theory and action

number nineteen

IN THIS ISSUE: GLEN COULTHARD ON RECOGNITION AND DECOLONIZATION ▣ YAVAR HAMEED ON RELATIONSHIPS OF RESISTANCE ▣ JOE BIEL ON AUTISTS AND ACTIVISM ▣ THOMAS CHIASSON-LEBEL & CHRISTIAN PÉPIN ON THE 2015 CUPE STRIKES ▣ DANIEL GUITERREZ, ANTJE DIETERICH & VICTOR HERTZFELD ON KURDISH AUTONOMY ▣ SHREYA GHIMIRE ON CASTE AND DALIT ACTIVISM ▣ BAIJAYANTA MUKHOPADHYAY ON CARE AS COLONIALISM ▣ ROUNDTABLES ON FOOD JUSTICE & ABOLITION AND REFORM ▣ BOOK REVIEWS & MORE...